Lakeland Laughter

IONICUS

Who was 'a small, withered, puckered, winking lady,
who never spoke'?

— *Mrs Wordsworth, described by Carlyle.*

Whose face had a sallow colour that 'speaks rather
of the rude and boistrous greeting of
mountain-weather'?

— *Wordsworth, as noted in Blackwood's Magazine
(1819).*

Who had 'a wide mouth, thick lips and not very
good teeth, longish, loose-growing, half-curling,
rough black hair'?

— *Coleridge, observed by Dorothy Wordsworth
(1802).*

Who was 'as manashable as a bairn, and was a bairn
that needed manashing until the end'?

— *Hartley Coleridge, who lived at Nab Cottage.*

Lakeland Laughter
NATIVE WIT AND HUMOUR

by

W R Mitchell

**(with the co-operation
of Radio Cumbria)**

Foreword by The Rt Hon Viscount Whitelaw

**CASTLEBERG
1993**

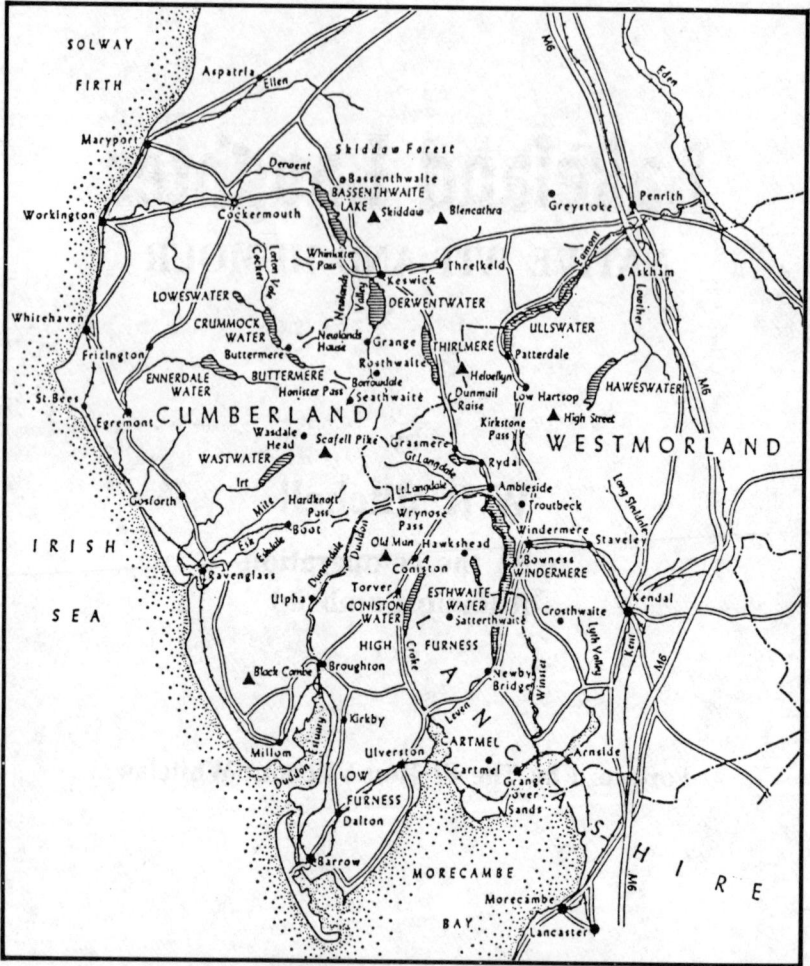

THE PRE-1974 LAKE DISTRICT.

Published by Castleberg, 18 Yealand Avenue, Giggleswick,
Settle, North Yorkshire, BD24 0AY

Typeset in Clearface and printed by J W Lambert & Sons,
Station Road, Settle, North Yorkshire, BD24 9AA

ISBN: 1 871064 01 5

4

Contents

Illustrations

Cartoons by IONICUS

Front cover from a painting by Edward Jeffrey

Back cover: photograph of 'Gondola' steaming on
              Coniston Water *(W R Mitchell)*

Map of Lakeland: Alan G Hodgkiss

'Last time I sweat like this, I had a
prize coo at t'Westmorland Show.'

Foreword

by

The Rt. Hon. The Viscount Whitelaw, KT, CH, MC.

I AM DELIGHTED to contribute a foreword for a book which is closely connected with Cumbrian life and, in particular, Cumbrian humour. Both are very special, and both have encouraged me at difficult times during the thirty-eight years of my life in Cumbria.

When I first became a Member of Parliament for Penrith and the Border, life in the country districts was local and lonely. Many farms and houses had no electricity, and I met farming families in outlying areas who had never even been into Carlisle. What is more, some spoke only with a strong Cumbrian dialect, which was very difficult to understand.

When one reflects on those days, it is encouraging to think how much Radio Cumbria has enriched the lives of those who live in these outlying areas. This book, full of so much humour, will entertain particularly the many families who remember those days and, indeed, will amuse us all.

A Cumbrian M.P. was accustomed to receiving some very blunt replies. I remember one particular experience when I met a farmer near Silloth. He was enraged at the proposed closure of the railway.

'How often did you use the railway?' I asked.

'I have never been on it in my life—what a silly question to ask me.'

To which I said: 'Well if you have never been on it why are you so keen to retain it?'

'Because every morning at 12 o'clock I know it is time for my dinner. The train passes at that time.'

'Perhaps you had better get a watch,' I replied.

'A very stupid suggestion—I shall never vote for you again,' was the answer.

Introduction

THE production of this book is a testimony to the power of Local Radio. As a result of a competition in Alan Smith's programme on BBC Radio Cumbria, almost three hundred amusing tales were sent in by listeners. Most of them were good enough to be included in this book.

BBC Radio Cumbria, through its news and information programmes, chronicles the day-by-day life of the county in a serious and authoritative way. But the station also has a sense of humour and offers entertainment. As a result, it has long attracted more listeners than any other radio station heard in Cumbria apart from Radio 1, which aims for a very different, much younger audience.

BBC Radio Cumbria is as much a social service as a public service. Its presenters are welcomed as friends into many a Cumbrian home. For the lonely, they may be the only 'regular visitors'.

When the radio station was about to open in November, 1973, as BBC Radio Carlisle, a questionaire was widely distributed. One of the questions was: 'How could you contribute to BBC Radio Carlisle?'

One of the answers which came back said: 'By door-to-door collections'.

NIGEL HOLMES
(Senior Producer)

Those Radio Times...

1922 Nov 1 Introduction of the 10 shilling radio licence
          14 BBC broadcasts begin from London
          15   ,,   ,,   Manchester
      Dec 23   ,,   ,,   Newcastle
1923 Mar 23   ,,   ,,   Glasgow
1927 Easter Day First broadcast from Cumberland (service
      from Carlisle Cathedral)
1934 First liner launch broadcast from Vickers, Barrow
1943 Empire Service short wave transmitters opened at
      Skelton, near Penrith
1956 First television broadcast from Cumberland
      (HM The Queen opened Calder Hall nuclear power
      station)
1957 First BBC studio in Cumberland (Opened in Bullough's
      store, Carlisle)
1958 VHF/FM radio transmissions begin from Sandale mast,
      near Wigton
1958 Cumbrian and Manx edition of radio news begins
1968 BBC Local Radio (forerunner of BBC Radio Carlisle)
      begins in Durham
1973 Nov 24 BBC Radio Carlisle opens (eight hours a day)
1980 Mar 28 Opening of first television studio in Cumbria
1982 May 22 BBC Radio Carlisle becomes
              BBC Radio Cumbria
          25 First transmission from Barrow studios to
              South Cumbria
1986 Opening of FM/VHF transmitters (carrying BBC Radio
      Cumbria) in Kendal and Windermere
1993 Mar 1 Opening of new BBC Radio Cumbria studios
              in Carlisle and first local radio broadcasts in
              stereo

A Cumbrian Sense of Humour

HAS the Cumbrian a sense of humour?

Undoubtedly, but he or she does not parade it, preferring a witty remark to a rambling tale which has already been heard before. The Cumbrian shows considerable patience while waiting for the 'punch line' of someone else's tale which has already been up and down the dale a score of times.

It's the 'one-liner' which draws the biggest laugh. When a doctor slipped his thermometer under the tongue of a normally garrulous farmer's wife, who for several minutes was unable to speak, her husband remarked: 'How mich does yan o' them cost?'

The sight of a briefly-clad woman rambler walking down Borrowdale prompted a villager to say to his neighbour: 'I dean't knaw why t'midges bothers to bite thee an' me when there's tasty bits like yon.'

It was in Borrowdale I heard the brief tale of the man who emigrated to Canada and returned to visit friends and relatives some thirty years later. One of his old cronies asked: 'Bin on thee holidays?'

Cumbrian humour is not like the Scottish type of tale perfected by Harry Lauder which leans heavily on a few national characteristics, introducing intemperate men and their long-suffering 'wee wifies'.

Nor is it the slap-on-the-back, belly-laugh humour of the industrial towns of Lancashire and Yorkshire.

Cumbrians tend to talk quietly, with a little bit of the Scottish burr about their speech. Those living in Lakeland certainly need a sense of humour in a beautiful but austere district of chilly soils

11

which is watered by over a hundred inches of rain annually. A villager, calling at the pub, was served with a pint of ale. Eventually, the affable landlord said: 'Looks like rain.' The villager looked at his glass and said, dolefully: 'Aye—and it tastes like it.'

The old-style Cumbrian was sparing with money; he was also economical in the use of words. A traveller representing a soft drinks company visited a grocer's shop and asked: 'Owt?' The answer was: 'Nowt.'

On occasion, a conversation was allowed to run-on. In Eskdale, the talker digressed when a lile, brown, long-bodied dog was seen and he commented: 'Some folk say that yon's a dash-hound. I'd call it a reight mis-fit.'

The urban sense of humour is keen. At the ever-breezy Barrow-in-Furness, 'thou can allus tell a native-born; he holds on to his cap when he comes to a corner.' It can be picturesque. A parishioner told a new, and bemused, Vicar: 'Thoo'll do aw reet as lang as thoo keeps t'cart on t'wheels.'

The Cumbrian is clannish, more so before 1974 when the Boundary Commission played fast-and-loose with old county loyalties and natives of Cumberland, Westmorland and Lancashire north of t'Sands were converted into an amorphous mass.

Humour and wit thrived in the days when every little dale—and there are lots of them in Cumbria—was a kingdom unto itself. The old lady, born, reared, wed and widowed near Buttermere was taken by car to the top of Honister Pass and, looking into the next dale, said: 'I nivver knew t'world was sae big.'

Folk at Grasmere and Ambleside, in Owd Westmorland, nivver trusted strangers from the north and said, feelingly: 'Nowt good comes ower t'Raise.' It presumably applied to those travelling the other way, as in the case of mother and child who were on a bus trip from Grasmere to Keswick. A road sign stood at the county border. Mother said to her son: 'We're now in Cumberland.' Her small son replied: 'We're not—we're in t'bus.'

A man who was asked what he would feel like if the boundary was changed and he found himself in a new county, simply said: 'I couldn't stand t'climate.'

The Cumbrian comes in differing sizes, shapes and mannerisms, in part dictated by the sort of country in which he was born and reared. There are the Lakers proper, in an area that's all fells and watter. In some places, a man had yan leg shorter than t'other through walking on steep fellsides.

The Plainsfolk, from North Cumberland, go in for ploughing and combine harvesting against the silvery Solway, beyond which lie the blue hills of Scotland. The area is much more fertile than the dales. A rabbit-catcher said: 'There's a place near Wigton where there's so many rabbits, you've to pull a couple out of a burrow before you can git t'ferret in.'

When an old chap saw a combine harvester for the first time he marvelled at the ingenious mechanics of it and remarked: 'Chap 'at invented yon hed more na nits in his heeard.'

A story from the village of Abbeytown is recounted by John Hurst, Editor of the *Cumberland and Westmorland Herald,* who is a native of that place. A man called Caleb rejoiced in his great strength and said he could lift anything. Someone remarked: 'See if thoo can lift thisel in a swill [small basket used in agriculture]. Caleb tried hard to lift himself and later reported: 'Ah wad a dun, but just afore I manished it, t'bottom came oot o' t'swill.'

John Dalton, discoverer of the atomic theory, was born at Eaglesfield, near Cockermouth, and one of the commemorative tablets was inscribed 'John Dalton, DCL LLD.' It was generally understood in the area that the initials meant 'Decent Civil Lad, Lang Legged Divvel'.

The North Pennine folk, around Alston, living at an elevation of over 1,000 feet, speak with soft musical voices, when you'd expect—knowing their bleak terrain—that they would caw like a lot o' crows. You must have heard the story of a visitor who, having shown interest in a large flock of rooks, which are members of the crow family, was told: 'Them's crows. We have a name for each of 'em.' The visitor marvelled. 'Aye,' continued the Pennine man, 'we calls 'em all crows.'

Around Carlisle, there's now (after centuries of warfare) a strong Anglo-Scottish flavour. My wife has a cousin who farms near the border, and sometimes plays whist—one week in England and the next week in Scotland. At one time they'd be clobbering each other, but now they're passing round the tea and scones and asking about the health of each other's families.

A Cumbrian woman who married a Scotsman was heard to say: 'My son takes after me—he likes to save money. But he also takes after his father—it's my money he saves!'

Around the Lake District are the towns—Penrith, Whitehaven and its neighbours, Barrow, Ulverston and Kendal, where a farmer is said to have taken his son and, stopping in Stricklandgate, to have rapped his stick against the pavement, saying: 'I telled thee nobody ploughs in Kendal. Grund's too hard.'

Two old Cumbrians met in Kendal market. They had not seen each other for many years. One said: 'I've nivver forgitten thee. When t'*Westmorland Gazette* comes, first thing I look for is t'obituaries—to see if thou's deeard.'

Lancashire was once very proud of its wedge-shaped piece of Lakeland, which took in Coniston, where (so 'they' say) the farmers count the sheep by a strange and laborious process: 'Yan, tean, tedderte, medderte, pimp, sethra, lethera, hovera, dovera, dik...'

Barrow once boasted of 'steam trams'. They were familiar to an old character, nicknamed Swattem, who was treated to a day out at Morecambe, where he saw an 'electric tram'. He commented: 'Y'kna they beats owt—Ah've sin a tram ga wi 'osses an ah've sin em ga wi' steam, but it were fust time ah'd sin a tram go wi' a fishing rod.'

Lancashire's strangest route was that Oversands from Lancaster to Grange. No one dawdles on that route. When the tide is out, fishermen wearing blue ganseys set off to collect shrimps, with tractors, trailers and beam nets. It's a healthy life. One of them told me: 'They had to shoot somebody to start a cemetery.'

A favourite Lakeland story is of the folk who lived at a remote house 'back o' Skidda'.' This resident family did not even see a postman, who went only as far as Dash Farm.

'Well, t'folks at Skiddaw House had a lile lad. He'd nivver sean naebody but his fadder and mudder. Imagine that. Yan day, a man come oop to t'hoose and t'lile lad, he run in till his mudther and says: 'Eh mudther, I'se that fleyt [freightened]. There's summat cooming oop to to'door, and I don't kna whativver it is—but it's a thing like oor fadther!'

It has been my good fortune for almost 45 years to have been associated with *Cumbria* magazine, for forty years as Editor, and to have shared in the rich informal fellowship of fell and dale. Among the many friends who are 'no longer with us', as they say, was Jack O'Connor of Kendal.

Jack was fond of telling about the hungry lile lad who went into a grocer's shop and asked for half a pennorth o' brokken biscuits.

15

The kind old lady behind the counter filled his cap with broken biscuits then, impulsively, handed back the halfpenny. Said the lad: 'Another half pennorth of biscuits, please.'

Jack also mentioned the Kendalian who was converted by the Methodists. He went to a prayer meeting and confessed: 'Some folk think I'm cracked.' The leader of the meeting promptly prayed: 'Crack a few more, Lord; there's plenty of work for 'em down here.'

Cumbrians are fond of 'a drop o' summat', though it was going too far when, offered a flask, the recipient was expecting whisky and it turned out to be summat else. The owner of the flask, noticing the bemused look on the face of his friend, said: 'It's claret.' The Cumbrian screwed up his face, then said: 'If yon stuff cost owt, it was too dear!'

Much of the humour concerns food. It's your stomach 'at 'ods your back up. The lad who was invited to a meal at a Methodist household was surprised when heads were bent to murmur the grace. So he asked: 'What are yer aw talken to yer puddings for?'

At a time of gloom and despondency, when every newspaper and every news programme on radio and television is a doleful recital of wars, rumours of war, muggings and rapes, it was stimulating when Radio Cumbria agreed to take part in a competition for the best local tales. The old Cumbrian spirit lives on through many amusing stories.

An appeal for tales brought in an almost overwhelming response, and many of the tales appear in this book, which also includes stories from my own collection, plus some of the radio talks I have given on Saturday mornings when I have stressed the lighter side of life.

The result, *Lakeland Laughter,* continues a happy association with broadcasting in Carlisle which began in the 1960s when I wrote a script for a documentary on John Peel. The programme was produced by Richard Kelly, who mustered some local talent, including the choral group Men of the Fells.

Lakeland Laughter is not the first time tales about the district have been assembled. William Dickinson published some in his *Cumbriana* (1875).

Dickinson told of Tommy Stamper, who lived near Penrith and sent his young son to school. After a few months, Tommy was asked by a neighbour how the lad was getting on with his lessons. The reply was: 'He's stickin' at K. I knew he would be a dulbert, for his fadder was yan.'

The fellside farming communities were acknowledged to produce plain, sensible, hard-working lasses who made excellent wives. A master mason said to his son: 'Divvent git hod o' thur feckless dris't up [dressed-up] things about here; bit gang thy ways up amang t'fells and find thissen a lass 'at's fit to make a wife on.'

Another Dickinson tale is of a raw youth, who was being trained as a page in a big house in West Cumberland. He wanted to know if finger glasses were to be placed on the table at an approaching dinner party. What he actually said was: 'Is t'company gaan to wesh thersels today?'

Then and in later times, a Cumbrian has never been over-awed by authority, though 'Gweordie' Rayson of Brigham, near Cockermouth, was going a little too far when he met Bishop Williams, who was wearing his formal attire, complete with gaiters. Looking at the gaiters, Gweordie said: 'Hesta biked it?'

Gweordie was noted for his 'howlers', remarking that the Vicar was pleased there were 'mair folk on t'electric roll'. He called a confirmation service a 'conflamation'.

William Dodd, of Penrith, told me about two brothers who lived on their own. Each referred to the other as 'yan of us'. In due course, one man knocked on the neighbour's house door and, when the summons was answered, said: 'Can yer kum—yan of us is deed.'

We don't waste words in Cumbria. I asked a man who was standing near a fork of the road, which of the two ways would take me to the main road to Kendal. He said: 'Ayther on 'em.'

'Which is the better road?' I inquired. He simply said: 'Nayther on 'em.'

See what I mean about the Cumbrian's sparse but effective use of words?

Cumbrian Speyks

SAID to a poor schoolmaster at Workington: 'She'll lick a lean thibel (porridge stick) 'at weds thee.'

A farmer, asked if his son had started courting, said: 'Aye—and he's fair fierce.'

Of a hill shepherd who was no longer able to walk uphill: 'A rotten sheep will run downhill.'

Uttered by Buttonsticks (a West Cumberland character): 'How soon it gets late'; and 'there's folk deeing (dying) now as 'av nivver deed (died) afore!'

Farmer to visiting schoolteacher: 'We doan't hev much eddication up here—we hev to use our brains.'

A person who was work-shy, who feigned illness or made much of a slight ailment, was known at Abbeytown as 'a good-like badly body.'

Of a gossip who was fond of elaborating on local tales: 'If she's not oot fishin', she's mending her nets.'

Of a Carlisle man who married late in life: 'He hesn't lang to go if it doesn't turn out reet.'

Langdale farmer in foggy weather: 'I'se just bin on t'fell. Fog were so thick, if I hedn't knawn where I was, I wouldn't have known where I were.'

Sexton, commenting on small population in a Lakeland parish: 'Give me six full days and I'd bury t'lot.'

Of an inquisitive Grasmerian: 'She taks meear pleasure i' what she sees i' t'kirkyard nor what she hears in' t'kirk.'

Old advert for Ratty, the Eskdale Railway: 'Why see Naples and die? See Eskdale and live.'

A local called out to a man who was exercising two trail hounds: 'Hey, Jonty—which end of t'chee-an [chain] does ta think t'brains is on?' [Which of the hounds is the most intelligent].

Whitehaven man, talking about air travel: 'Thoo can tek me as fast and as high as thoo likes so lang as I ev ya foot on t'groond.'

A Borrowdale man, telling a friend about his strange-looking breeches: 'T'wife's new-foresided 'em wi' t'backsides fra a pair of auld 'uns. I can't tell whedder I'se gaan backwerts or forrets.'

Stories From Radio Listeners

IN THE competition organised with BBC Radio Cumbria for the best Cumbrian tales, I was impressed by the large number of examples of humour with a contemporary setting. Few people who submitted entries had recourse to the hoary old tales.

I thank everyone who sent in a story. Examples of Cumbrian wit and humour enlivened a murky January, during which many tales were read out on the air.

Every entry was worthy of a prize, but only seven could qualify. In selecting the winners, I looked for amusing stories which had a true Cumbrian flavour, were succinct—and made me laugh. Reading the whole collection has given me a face massage!

The Winner:

Mrs Guy Pearson, Borderside, Crosthwaite, via Kendal, sent the following story:

Some years ago, the local policeman called at our farm to check the current gun licence firearms certificate which my husband holds to shoot vermin, etc. The policeman was sitting with us, having a cup of coffee, when my husband was asked: 'Do you shoot much?' Before anyone could answer, my daughter piped up with: 'No, but he aims at a lot.'

The Six Runners-up:

(1) *(Mrs) D Mackenzie, 325 Pennine Way, Carlisle.*

Many years ago, my young brother was going on a school trip to the Lake District. Before leaving, my mother said: 'You'd better go to the toilet first.' My brother replied: 'It's OK, mum—I'll just go behind a mountain.'

(2) *Ros Robinson, The Restaurant, 51 Castlegate, Penrith.*

A couple came into the restaurant. The gentleman ordered a fillet steak. I asked him how he liked it to be cooked, expecting him to answer with the usual 'rare', 'medium', etc. He said: 'Enough so's the vet can't revive it.'

(3) *Kath Little, 102 Vancouver Road, Eastrigg, Annan.*

An old Bewcastle couple visited Carlisle. The woman visited a posh toilet, which was much better than the outside privy at home. Excitedly, she reported to her husband on her experience: 'Ee, lad, thoo's nivver seen owt like it. There a grand seat t'sit on. Then thoo pulls t'chain and there's just enuff watter left t'wash thee hands.'

(4) *Mrs May Armstrong, 2 High Wray Cottage, Ambleside.*

An old man was recalling how he nearly drowned in Windermere. 'I had a varra near squeak. I was up to me ankles.' His friend said: 'Thoo couldn't drown if thoo was nobbut up to thee ankles.' The old man simply remarked: 'I was wrang side up.'

(5) *Kenneth Robinson, Burnain Hall, King Meaburn, Penrith.*

At Penrith Auction Mart. Auctioneer: 'Won't somone start the bidding for this very small but healthy calf?'

Voice from outside the ring: 'Not unless thoo sells it wi' a butterfly net to tak it yam wid.'

(6) *Steve Kellett, Old School House, Finsthwaite, Ulverston.*

A farmer, working his dog without much success, finally gave up and shouted: 'Come here—and I'll ga mesell.'

Some of the Remaining Stories

A little lad returned to Dalton C of E School after being poorly. One of the dinner ladies asked: 'Have you had chickenpox?' He replied: 'No. Fish fingers and chips.'
C Bailey, 1 Cumberland Close, Millom.

I overheard two elderly ladies talking on the bus. They were discussing recent alterations such as the building of the Civic Centre and Lanes. One lady remarked that the best thing was when they moved the Castle back to provide more room for the traffic.
(Mrs) Pat Douglas, 62 Winscale Way, Morton Park, Carlisle.

In the old days, farm men had to work hard all day, with no overtime pay. At the end of a particularly long day, the farmer said to his man: 'He was a good chap who invented Bed.' The young man replied: 'Aye—but he was even better who invented Night—otherwise we'd have never got to it.'
(Mrs) J P Harker, 7 Greenwood Close, Thursby.

A farmer told his man that he was going to the auction mart. He mentioned a number of jobs to be done 'after you've turned that hay.' The farm man asked when he had to clear the snow, whereupon the farmer asked: 'What snow?' Said the lad: 'It's bound to be snowing by t'time I git through that lot!'
(Mrs) M Cowling, Greenhouse Farm, Lowca, near Whitehaven.

The old man who offered to help at haytime was given a job stacking bales while the younger end threw them up to him. One bale hit the old man and knocked him down the other side of the stack. When the youngsters rushed round, he was brushing himself down. They inquired if he was all right. 'Aye, lads,' replied the old man. 'I was coming down anyway.'

Jennie Sherwen, 83 Meadowfield, Gosforth, Seascale, CA20 1HU.

One of two farmers at the auction mart was looking glum. His friend asked him the reason. He replied: 'I'm bothered about sex.' The other retorted: 'Sex at your age. Don't be daft.' The reply was: 'I'm not daft. You'd be bothered if you had two fields o' taties and no sex to put 'em in.'

Bob Walker, 25 Minster Close, Workington.

A man returned to his native Cumbrian village after many years of exile. Everything and everyone seemed to have changed. He then saw an old chap with a familiar face. 'Do you know me?' he demanded. 'I was one of the Robinsons who lived down that lane.' The old chap thought for a while, then said: 'I remember 'em now. Was it thee, or thi brother, who died?'

(Mrs) M Hutchinson, 4 Main Road, Endmoor, Kendal, LA8 0EU.

One day a friend's car would not start. He asked his brother to look at it. The brother obliged. After examining the engine, he remarked: 'Does'ta see yon nut there—well, it's missing!'

Sandra Dixon, 1 Romney Gardens, Kendal, LA9 5TR.

A Lakeland farmer visited the bank with a milk churn which was full of £10 and £5 notes. He asked an assistant to count them. The figure was £45,000 precisely. The farmer, not satisfied, asked for

a re-count. When the same figure was announced he said: 'Sorry, lad—I must have brought t'wrang churn.'
George Bailey.

A lady rang the fire service and reported a fire. 'Will you come quickly?' she added. A fireman asked: 'Where is the fire?' to be told: 'It's in my house.' 'How do we get to it?' The lady sighed and said: 'Haven't you got a fire engine?'
Dennis Douglas, 86a George Street, Whitehaven.

Years ago, I was making fancy dresses for my children when my daughter began to praise me. As she spoke, my head seemed to get bigger and bigger. Then she took a deep breath and said: 'Mam, you haven't many brains, but you've lots and lots of common sense.' My head quickly went back to size.
Betty Lloyd, 14 Orchard Road, Wigton, CA7 9JL.

A farm man who was about to get married said: 'I'll git her a weshing tub and a leuking glass. She can either wesh for a living or watch hersel' starve to deeth.'
(Miss) Annie E Lowthian, 7 Sockbridge Drive, Tirril, Penrith, Cumbria, CA10 2JP.

Harking back to my Young Farmers' Club days, I recalled one of the lads saying (after being annoyed by someone): 'Eh, if I'd had a gun, I would have brayed [hit] him wi' it.'
Pauline Scott, Winder Farm, Dearham, Maryport.

During a party at a house in a remote Lakeland valley, where the heating did not extend to the outside privy, the hostess went to each of the female guests in turn and inquired if they wanted to use the toilet. Eventually, she was heard saying to her husband:

'Doesn't anybody want to go to t'toilet. I just hate sitting on a cold seat!'

Alan Marsh, Cooper Engraving, Ecclerigg, near Windermere.

My father-in-law was taken, as a child, to have tea with friends near Cleator Moor. Being a Barrovian, he didn't understand all that was said. The farmer's wife could see he was a bit shy about helping himself at table, so she pushed a plate of scones towards him and said: 'Reach to and tak' yan.' Little Hughie was quite confounded.

(Mrs) W Smith, 72 Furness Park Road, Barrow-in-Furness, LA14 5PX.

A small boy asked his Mum if we come from dust and go back to dust when we die. 'Yes, son,' she replied. 'Well,' said the small boy, 'there's somebody coming or going under my bed.'

(Mrs) F Case, Duddon Vista, The Hill, Millom, LA18 5HD.

A young couple asked the Vicar to baptise their baby daughter. At the service, he said: 'Name this child.' Mother said: 'Spindonna'. Afterwards, the Vicar said he had never heard that name before. The proud mother replied: 'Never heard of Mary. It's pinned on her.'

(Mrs) S Hindmarch, 1 Burnbanks, Penrith, CA10 2RW.

Rene Roberts autographed a copy of her book on the day it was published and I gave the book to Dad when I got home. He asked: 'Did you pay for this?' I nodded. 'Well, you shouldn't have,' he replied. 'Somebody's written their name in it already.'

(Miss) Alma Graham, 1 High Green, Hayton, Aspatria.

Overheard in a Florists' shop:
Florist: 'Now this potted plant is a really good buy.'

'I reckon I'm as lish as a cat
in a tripe shop.'

Customer: 'Goodbye to £3.'
Kenneth Robinson, Burnain Hall, Kings Meaburn, Penrith.

A party of young men from Wigton were at Worthing, on the South Coast. A local asked them in what part of England this place called Wigton might be found. One of the Cumbrians said: 'Half way between Micklethwaite and Waverton.' Where else?
(Mrs) Muriel Douglas, 38 Glebe Close, Dalston, Carlisle.

There was a queue at the fish shop. A young man came rushing in, going straight to the front. An old lady asked him what he was doing, adding: 'Does ta like fish?' He said he loved fish. 'Well, lad,' said the old lady, 'there a 'plaice' at back o' t'queue for thee.'
(Mrs) M Broatch, 11 Meadow Road, Mirehouse, Whitehaven.

The Nether Kellet television transmitter had failed. Two women, who were chatting in an Ulverston shop, were concerned that they would miss 'Eastenders'. A third one chipped in with these consoling words: 'We'll be aw right 'cos our Jack has set t'video on 'record' and we can watch t'programme tomorrow.'
Norman Foster, 15 Chestnut Grove, Ulverston.

Our little grandson Alfred, who is of farming stock, won his first pre-school sportsday race, but ducked beneath the finishing tape. Asked why, he replied: 'I thought it was an electric fence.'
He went on to gain three rosettes that day.
June Sherwen, Egremont.

A few years ago, an elderly neighbour died. My daughter asked her aunt if she would be going to the funeral. She said: 'Nay, won't bother. She waint be going ta mine.'
Eunice Dixon, 1 Romney Gardens, Kendal, LA9 5TR.

A small boy ran into the house, sobbing, and said to his mother that Dad had hit his thumb with the hammer. Mother said: 'You shouldn't be crying, lad; you should have laughed.' The lad replied, between sobs: 'I did.'
(Mrs) G Burrough, Mealo Hill Farm, Allonby, Maryport.

During the war we attended barn dances in the villages. The farm lads, raw young boys, stood in one group and us girls stood opposite them, waiting for an invitation to dance. One night, a rosy-faced young man came across the floor, put his hand out to me, and said: 'Hello—can I borrow thee carcass?' I followed him on to the floor like a lamb to the slaughter.'
Jennie Sharpe, 42 Heron Hill, Kendal, LA9 7JD.

My Dad, a farmer, used to shout this every Monday morning when awakening my brother and cousin: 'Come on, lads. T'day efter tomorrow is t'middle of t'week—and there's nowt done yet!'
Janet Brownrigg, Scar Sykes, Newbiggin-on-Lune, Kirkby Stephen.

A farmer constantly reminded his estate agent about a promise to provide some new doors for his calf pens, saying: 'When's ah ganta git them doors for me cauf hulls?' The agent said he knew about them; 'they are in my book.' The farmer exclaimed: 'Beuk! beuk! What's t'good o' them int'beuk—it's on t'hulls where ah want 'em.'
(Mrs) Ivy Laycock, 42 Sandylands Road, Kendal, LA9 6EU.

'Buttonsticks', a character in Whitehaven pre-war, was talking about a large crowd at a Church funeral, adding: 'If they had all got in, it wouldn't have held half of them.'
Barbara Benn, Montford, Braystones Road, Beckermet.

I am the RSPCA Inspector for West Cumbria. I was looking for a farm in the Seascale area which I could not find, so I stopped at another farm for directions. I asked the farmer if he could help me. 'Aye,' he said, 'but if I were you, I wouldn't start from here.'
Paul Wilson, 68 Leathwaite, Whitehaven, CA28 7UG.

My father, John Cross, who was Whitehaven born and bred, told me that when he and mother were courting on kells 'tops' one day, father made a reference to 'scopping styans owert dyke.' My mother, who is a Yorkshire lass, did not have a clue what he meant until she was struck on the head by a 'styan'. Father then offered a translation of the dialect: throwing stones over the embankment. Mother still laughs and says this was her introduction to Cumbria.
Nick Cross, Duke Street, Southport, Lancs.

The River Kent was in full flood. A man rushed into the pub and said: 'Hey, Joe, thee hen-hut's just gone floating doon t'river.' Joe replied: 'Nay, it can't hev. I've getten t'key in me pocket.'
(Mrs) Marjorie Forsyth, 10 Anchorite Place, Kendal.

Some years ago I had a lift with a local farmer/milkman. I sat in his van while he delivered milk to a small firm, where a workman was in the yard with a noisy pressure hose. They exchanged a few words and the milkman roared with laughter. He came back to his van and climbed in with the words: 'Don't know what he said; it were summat, likely.'
Jill Aldersley, Archway Cottage, North Road, Ambleside, LA22 9DT.

The dustbin man was doing his rounds. He bumped into an old lady who was coming up the path. 'Where's your bin, missus?' 'I've

just been to Co-op for a bit of shopping.' 'No, where's your wheelie bin?' 'I've just told you; I've been shopping.'
John Tyson, 50 Lime Tree Road, Ulverston.

An elderly man being driven to a remote dalehead farm on a very hilly route was being badly shaken and said he would 'give five pounds to be out of this.' The unfeeling Jehu replied: 'Keep thee brass. Ye'll mebbe be oot for nowt afoore we git to t'far end.'
from 'Lakeland Memories' by George Seatree, JP.

Haymaking used to be much slower than it is now. Farmers worked from dawn to dusk. The young farm lads, wanting to take their girls dancing on a Saturday night, prayed for rain as follows:

Lord, if it be in Thy power;
Send down a shower
About aif past fower.

Willow Taylor, Stony Lane Cottage, Near Sawrey, Ambleside.

My farmer neighbour bought an Australian sheepdog at great expense. It was useless, jumping on the backs of the ewes, running off to the fells when unleashed and proving to be untrainable. I met him with the dog on a thick rope. 'Is it no better, then?' I asked. 'Ah the booger,' he said. 'Nae better? It's ten times nae better...'
T S Armstrong, South Ing, Bassenthwaite.

A farmer bought tickets for a draw from his neighbour. Some months later, they met and the first farmer asked the result: 'Wha won the draa then?' 'Oh—oor Jack. Wan't he lucky?' 'Wha wun t'second prize then?' 'Oor Joe. Wan't he lucky?' The speaker

gently pointed out that 'thaa's nivver paid me for t'tickets.' Whereupon the farmer remarked: 'Aye, aa knaa. Wan't aa lucky?'
T S Armstrong, South Ing, Bassenthwaite, Keswick.

At the funeral, the Vicar spoke very highly of the deceased. The grieving widow turned to her son and said: 'Come on, lad, we'd best get out of here. Ah think we've come to t'wrang funeral.'
Bob Wilson, 138 Kingstown Road, Carlisle, CA3 0AY.

When my little boy was five, his Daddy and I were getting ready to go to a funeral and we were explaining that Nana was looking after him for the day. He asked if he could come with us. When we said he couldn't, he thought for a while, then said: 'Why are children not invited to Dead Weddings?'
Gillian Wren, Lambrigg, Foxfield Road, Broughton-in-Furness.

While working as a dinner lady at school, I asked the head of the table why some infants had gone out to play without eating all their dinners. The lad, a farmer's son, replied: 'They're like a flock o' yows. When yan ga's, they aw ga.'
(Mrs) Sheila Percival, Shannan Brae, High Street, Morland, Penrith, CA10 3AS.

A Grasmere hotel porter who had loaded the heavy luggage, settled his departing guests on the stage coach, wrapped the rug around their knees but still hadn't received a tip. Throwing all caution to the wind, he said: 'By the way, when you get home and find you've lost your purse, you didn't have it out here!'
David Scott, Briarways, Spooner Vale, Windermere.

My favourite character is the old farmer who, when asked what the weather was going to do, always gave the same reply (after much consideration): 'Well—it'll either rain or go dark afore morning.'
(Mrs) M Hutchinson, 4 Main Road, Endmoor, Kendal.

Tourist: 'Where does this road go to?'
Farmer: 'I doan't knaw that it gangs anywheer. It's allus here when I come past.'
May Armstrong, 2 High Wray Cottages, High Wray, Ambleside, LA22 0JE.

The village nosey-parker, when talking to a Cumbrian farmer, said: 'I hear that Owd Harry's died.' 'Aye.' 'I'll bet he left a fair bit.' 'Aye, he did—he left the lot!'
(Mrs) Pam Whittaker, Fellbeck, 5 South Cres., Windermere.

Recently, my husband visited the sales in Carlisle to buy a new cap. After trying several on, he finally decided on one. The young assistant said: 'Is that the one you are going to buy?' For some moments, my husband looked at the upturned cap and said: 'Nay, lad, I'm taking a collection!'
(Mrs) Anne Balmer, 134 Houghton Road, Carlisle, CA3 0LD.

A junior school teacher was appointed to a rural school and on the first day she sketched a picture of the sheep and asked the class to identify it. There were blank faces. Then she asked Young Tom if he had any idea. With a face puckered up through concentration, he said: 'Well, miss, t'front end looks like a Herdwick and t'back-end like a Swaledale.'
Bryan Bond, 1 Longacre Close, Cragg Bank, Carnforth.

We stopped to stroke a dog being exercised by an old lady and we asked her if it was a dog or a bitch. The old lady replied: 'No, it's a good dog.' We later discovered its name was—Betty.

Dorothy Pooley, 13 Briar Bank, Cockermouth.

On a busy day, when time was at a premium, my Nan—a farmer's wife—said: 'Heck, time goes on gingerbread wheels and pasty clogs.' Daft—but we all knew what she meant.

Anne Crawford, 17 Danes Road, Staveley, near Kendal.

This is a true story which took place in a village outside Carlisle in 1951 and was relayed to me by my mother. The elderly ladies had just had a talk on Civil Defence and how to cope if the atom bomb dropped on the area! Tea was made. One lady, who had no teeth, took a sandwich and after one bite, she opened it to see what meagre filling lay inside.

After a pause, she leaned forward and shouted to the lady responsible for making the sandwiches: 'Bantams again, Jeannie.' The very small bantam eggs were less than adequate.

Gill Melrose, 103 Burgh Road, Carlisle, CA2 7NB.

Overheard at a harvest festival in Christ Church, Penrith, two or three years ago. Two visitors were admiring the produce. *He:* 'I'd love to try one of those black grapes.' *She:* 'You'd get a shock if you did—they're damsons!'

Jeremy Godwin, 15 Drovers Lane, Penrith, CA11 9EP.

A man took his grandson to Church for the first time. The lad, surprised when the collection plate came round, said: 'You don't have to pay for me, Grandad—I'm not five yet.'

(Mrs) Muriel Hall, Easedale, Keld Head, Stainton, Penrith.

Twenty years ago, a family friend was teaching me to drive a car. He arrived at the house one afternoon, when I hadn't washed my youngest son's face ready for going out. Ted looked at Michael, who was sitting on the floor, and said: 'By gum, lad, there's mischief all over your face.' Michael (aged four and a-half) promptly replied: 'That's not mischief; it's blooming muck.'
Thelma Barton, 5 Kirkfield, Ambleside.

This story was told to me by a lady who is now 91 years old. She lived in Howgill, near Sedbergh. A girl was bringing her boy friend home for the first time. Mother, while laying the table for tea, put out the usual pint pots. The girl thought that for this special occasion there should be cups and saucers. Mother said: 'Nay—start as thou means to hod oot [carry on].'
(Mrs) I Raven, 8 Silver Howe Close, Kendal.

I once bought a chamber pot at Mr Barratt's shop (now the doctor's surgery). He put the pot into a hat box. 'There you are, madam,' he remarked, 'now everybody will think you've bought a new hat.'
F. Case, Duddon Vista, The Hill, Millom.

An old worthy called Barlow liked a pint or two. He was fond of saying: 'They can cure ham. They can cure kippers. But they can't cure Barlow.'
Steve Kellett, Old School House, Finsthwaite.

I was waiting in Tesco's pay queue when I heard a lady say to the cashier: 'I'll take that clothes line only if you think it will reach to the bottom of my garden.'
(Mrs) A Studholme, 3 Dean Street, Workington.

When my children were small, I did not like them to call adults by their Christian names. When a neighbour drove by, my son said: 'Look, mum, there's Derek.' I corrected him by saying, firmly: 'Mr Gallaway'. My son said: 'He's driving Derek's car.'
Edna Keighan, 10 Longlands Ave., Barrow-in-Furness.

Two old timers stood on a street corner as a funeral passed by. One inquired of the other whose funeral it was and he was told: 'It's someone from Flimby.' The first old timer asked: 'What did he die from then.' The other replied: 'I was told, but I can't remember. I do know it was nowt serious.'
(Mrs) Sally Burrow, 7 Ellerbeck Lane, Workington.

Two old Lakeland characters, looking at a vapour trail left across the sky by a passing jet aircraft, said: 'I wouldn't like to be up there, in t'seat next to chap who's driving yon.' His friend replied: 'Aye, and I wouldn't like to be up there wi'out 'im.'
David J Oldham, Archways, Rusland, Ulverston.

As a policeman at Windermere in 1969, I was on foot patrol in Bowness one lovely summer's day when I was approached by an American, the umpteenth tourist who wanted to know the location of the lake. I had dealt with many such inquiries, and the way to the lake was well signposted, so I said to him in my broadest Cumbrian twang: 'Tha' keeps walkin' down theer an' when thi 'at's floatin' thoo's in it!'
J Ernie Graham, Lonicera, Bay View, Millom.

A farmer's wife said to her husband: 'Why do you put my mother's photograph on the mantlepiece?' The farmer replied: 'It keeps the bairns away from the fire.'
W Stitt, 1 Waverley Terrace, Hawick, Roxburghshire.

Lighter Side of Cumbrian Life

Angling

A Pennine man who saw the sea for the first time remarked: 'It's nowt but watter.' He could look at plenty of water nearer home. Lakeland is twenty per cent watter, its scenic impact ranging from gurt lakes to bits o' becks.

An Edenvale blacksmith used to go fishing with his biggest hammer, which he brought down on likely stones, under the edge of which fish were in the habit of lying.

An angler who had spent the day trying to tempt the Eden trout remarked to his wife on his return home: 'It's a really good river for fish. I couldn't persuade any of 'em to leave.'

A poacher waited until the beck-watcher was in the pub before setting off to the riverside with gaff (hooked implement) and torch, intent on 'clicking' some salmon.

A man who fished openly with rod and line was approached by the new beck-watcher, who thought he had made a 'fair cop' when he deduced the man had no fishing licence. The angler reeled in. On the hook was—a potato. The beck-watcher, feeling sorry for him, moved on without another word. That evening, in the pub, the angler displayed a plate of freshly-caught trout.

Said the beck-watcher: 'Thoo didn't catch that lot wi' a potato.' The angler replied: 'Nay—I used t'spud to catch thee.'

Babies

The Rev A J Smith, Vicar of Levens, visited a parishioner whose wife had just had her umpteenth child. He complimented him on the blessed event and then commented on how unfortunate it was that the lady of the manor (The Hon. Mary Howard) was childless when she would dearly have loved to have a son.

The Vicar added: 'God never sends a mouth without providing a morsel therewith.' Said the father: 'Aye, but he sends t'mouth to one house an' t'morsel to anudder.'

A farmer's wife, telling her husband about a visit to a neighbouring farm, where a new baby (usually referred to as 'it') was to be found said: 'It's such a big lad, it bawls like a calf.'

Barbering

A barber's shop was a proper cal-oil (gossiping place). The barber was invariably a man of great wit. Charlie Murray, of Wigton, was fond of saying to a customer he was shaving: 'Is ta wearing a red tie?' If the reply was in the negative, Charlie said: 'I must ha' cut your throat, then.'

Bedtime

A Cumbrian who paid his first visit to London stayed at a large hotel and surprised the night staff by appearing in the early hours with a towel over one arm. He wanted to be directed to the kitchen, where—as at home—he would begin the day by having a wesh (wash).

A member of the night staff persuaded him to return to his room, mentioning that he would find a jug full of water and a bowl. He could have a wash there. 'Nay,' said the farmer, 'I've supped that!'

Many years ago, Tyson Rigg of Dearham was by trade a mole-catcher but also mended umbrellas and, on Sundays, appeared in Cumberland pulpits as a Methodist local preacher. Tyson visited the Keswick Convention and, knowing there was a dearth of accommodation, he booked a room early.

When the first day's services were over, he retired to bed. Much later, the landlord knocked at his bedroom door and asked how many men were in the bed. 'Ah've got some mair folks ta put up and I want to know hoo many's in theer.'

'Well,' Tyson replied, 'there's a mowdie catcher, an umbrella mender, a Methody preacher, Old Tyson Rigg a' Dearham and mesell.' The landlord, concluding there were already plenty of folk in that bed, left Tyson in peace.

Builders

The old churches and farms of Lakeland have a durability that defies the worst the weather can give. Some modern buildings are not quite as well built. When a new-starter in the building trade completed his first dwelling, one of the villagers said: 'Bungalow was t'reight name for yon place. Job was bungled frae start to finish.'

In the old days, builders rarely went by the clock. If it was fine, then work continued while there was enough light. The son of a small-time builder who was putting a new roof on to a house groaned when his father said they would continue to work by moonlight, so as to get a 'straight edge'.

Five minutes later, the son said to his dad: 'Thoo's gittin yon slate wrang side up. It's time we knocked off.' Father disagreed, saying: 'If it's light enough for thee to see it's wrang side up, we can carry on a bit longer...'

Buses

Buses were invading the minor roads of Cumbria in some numbers after the 1914-18 war. Two bus drivers who were debating about the length of their daily run to a certain village had to reckon with the fact that there were two ways of access. Which was the longest?

It was decided to put the matter to the test. One driver remarked: 'Thee ga yan way and I'll ga t'other way. Which on us gits to t'kirk fust can stick a cobble on t'wall.'

'Aw reet.' said his friend, 'and if I git theer fust, I'll knock it off.'

A conversation about music included mention of Malcolm Sargent. 'Who?' 'Malcolm Sargent, the conductor.' 'Oh, aye. Does he work for t'*Ribble?*'

You've possibly heard of the man employed on a double-decker bus staffed by a driver who also issued the tickets. The bus was involved in a bad accident, fortunately without loss of life, and the driver was asked what he was thinking about at the time. 'Nay,' he replied, 'I was upstairs takking t'money.'

Church

St Mary's, at Ambleside, has a steeple which tickles the passing clouds. Kendal parish church is one of the largest in England. Martindale Old Church, barn-like in size (and up to a point in appearance) is one of those dalehead kirks which drew support from families living at scattered farms.

The sermons were long. One Vicar who didn't know when to stop preaching, and who had poor eyesight, drawled on for such a length of time that members of his congregation sneaked out, one by one. The Verger, finding that only he and the Vicar remained, left the Church keys on the edge of the pulpit and said: 'Will ta lock up when thoo's finished?'

Life used to be all bed and work, so that when a Vicar visited one remote church, intent on taking a service there, he took two farming brothers by surprise. They were about to load a farm cart. 'Nay, vicar, thoo's come a day too soon,' said one. The Vicar insisted it was the right day. The other brother thought for a while, then exclaimed: 'T'parson's reet. Gang on wi' t'service.'

When Sir George Rose was dining with Lord Langdale, his host mentioned the tiny church in Langdale, of which he was patron, and remarked: 'It is no bigger than this dining room.' Sir George observed: 'And I'm sure the living is not half so good.'

A Church was either 'high' or 'low' in its type of service. The new Vicar at a 'low' church was very high-minded. One of his flock remarked: 'He hes us bobbing up and doon like a lot o' tappets.'

A country Vicar was often worried in case the Bishop, a notable scholar, should preach a sermon that none of his congregation could understand. When he arrived to take a special service, he was diplomatically advised that a simple message would be appreciated. The Bishop went too far. After the service, the Vicar asked a fell farmer what he thought of the sermon. He said: 'Aw reet. But wor yon chap ivver eddicated?'

With the number of Church adherents declining, a service might be attended by only a dozen folk. An old-time Vicar of Grasmere, watching heavy traffic on Dunmail Raise, said to his churchwarden: 'Nowadays, the straight and narrow path is the only one which has no traffic problems.'

A Vicar is consoled if the Sunday School is well-supported. He addressed the children about the Christian 'armour', such as the breastplate of righteousness. Mention was also made of the sword of truth. The Vicar questioned the children about which weapon St Paul said we must carry. A small boy said, brightly: 'The Axe of the Apostles'.

Climbing

Climbers take a lofty view of the world and refer to caving (disparagingly) as 'inverted mountaineering'. Pioneer climbers— who were known as 'tigers', possibly because of the long burns of hempen ropes on their bodies—visited Wasdale, ritualistically left their boots in rows, quaffed ale, smoked pipes and practiced climbing by scaling the outer walls of a local barn.

Local farmers sometimes wonder what all the fuss is about. One climber, fully kitted, asked the local man for permission to climb a formidable crag solo. Said the farmer: 'Thoo doesn't need ta go ti all that trouble. Just walk down to yon tarn—and doan't stop when thoo comes to t'watter!'

Stanley Watson, of Borrowdale, was fond of saying: 'The greater the firma, the less the terra.' Derwin Leighton told the story of 'climmers' who, having just climbed Cust's Gully, were told by the farmer: 'Why, I wouldn't caw that climmin'. Ah'd tek a horse an' cart up theear!'

Two youngsters, having climbed a difficult face, were so pleased with their efforts one of them remarked: 'If we go on like this, we'll soon be good enough to have ropes.'

If Lakeland climbers have their temple, it's the *Wasdale Head Hotel,* where the visitors book contained a brief note about Pillar Rock: 'Today I ascended the Pillar in three hours and found the rocks very soft.' A wag had written underneath: 'Today I descended the Pillar in three seconds—and found the rocks very hard!'

Clothing

> *I lives in a neat little cottage;*
> *I rents me a nice little farm;*
> *On Sundays I dresses me handsome;*
> *On Mondays I dresses me warm.*
> Catherine Gilpin (18th century).

Courting

'Walking out' and 'holding hands' have given way to driving off in a car and getting up to goodness-knows-what mischief on the back seat.

41

Having a car does spare a Lakeland suitor a tediously long walk. It did not altogether help the Newlands lad who courted a lass oot o' Wasdale, just a few miles ower t'tops but an almost endless journey by road. His fortitude paid off; the couple are now married.

Farmers tend to be a bit shy, even about talking of love. An Eskdale suitor who asked a farmer if he might marry his daughter was told: 'Aye—you can wed our Edna; but doan't mention it to her yet. Or she'll go an' tell ivverybody.'

A Cockermouth couple had been courting for fourteen years when the lady said: 'Isn't it time we were wed?' Her young man replied: 'Who'd 'ev us?'

In the Kendal area, the lady tried to rush matters and as her young man was returning from market with a piglet under each arm, she speeded ahead of him. 'What's t'matter?' he demanded. She thought he might want to kiss her. 'Nay, I've got me hands full o' pigs,' he said.

The lady looked coy as she remarked: 'I thought you might ask me to hold 'em.'

Dancing

Dancing is a vigorous activity in Cumberland. A person has to move in a lively fashion to keep up with the strains of fiddle and piano accordion.

Even so, John Keats, the poet, after walking from Keswick to Carlisle (1818), attended a dance and wrote: 'The difference between our country dances and these Scottish figures is almost the same as leisurely stirring a cup of tea and beating a batter pudding.'

It is said that at a Carlisle dance, an old-fashioned waltz was in progress when the man said to his partner: 'Can you reverse?' She replied: 'Are you getting dizzy?' 'Nay,' he remarked, 'you're unscrewing my wooden leg.'

Farming

You see farmers at their best when they're discussing stock at an auction mart or showing their prize animals at an agricultural show. At home they are apt to be pre-occupied with day-to-day work. Not until evening will they have time for a natter.

A visitor to Wescow, a hamlet near Threlkeld, admired the views of Naddle Fell and St John's Vale. Turning to the farmer, he complimented him on the view. The farmer said: 'Appen so—but it won't do t'wark [work].'

Which reminds me of the newly-hired lad who asked: 'What shall I hev to do?' The farmer said: 'Thou'll hev to wark, lad. I can do t'laiking [playing] misself.'

The Eskdale farmer who, having used up his stock of hay before the first flush of new grass appeared, turned his cows into the frost-stiffened fields. A neighbour questioned the wisdom of this move, observing that they had not much to eat. Said the farmer: 'I knaws that, but look at t'view they've getten.'

A long-bearded visitor to a Cumbrian farm had no response to his knocking on the door, so he slowly opened the door and peeped in—just as a farmer awoke from a deep sleep. He shouted: 'Who's backing a horse in here?'

Comes the day when the Cumbrian farmer feels he has to 'ease up'. A retired farmer who lived near Kendal returned home fairly late from the inn. As he climbed the stairs, his wife—who had been spring-cleaning aw day—called out from the bedroom: 'Mind you don't run into t'chest o' drawers on t'landing.' He replied: 'A's nut garn ta run.'

And always the generation gap is evident in the attitude of old and young to work. A Borrowdale farmer said to his young son: 'Folk o' your age don't knaw you're born. When I started wark, I'd to git up at five o'clock ivvery morn. And I thought nothing of it.'

Said the son: 'You were right, Dad, and I don't think much of it, either.'

Fell Country

I once stood with a Coniston man, looking towards the fells. He remarked: 'There's a terrible lot of unseen grund up theer!' Indeed.

Will Ritson, of *Wasdale Head Hotel,* listened while someone in a party of climbers headed by William Cecil Slingsby told about their getting lost in fell-top mist.

Said Will: 'Why! That's nowt! Ah can beat that mesell. Ah mind yance wid been hunting ower t'Ennerdale fells and hed kilt a great dog fox on t'Pillar Fell. He was running for t'bield [shelter] under t'crag, and Rattler gripped him afoor he gat intil t'whoal.

'Ah mind t'mist com doon and we could see nowt and wander't rownd and rownd, and laal Tom Nicholson, o' Branthwaite, says: 'It's nea use graping aboot like this. Let's mak doon teva Black Sail.'

'An afoor we could see owt to ken t'road by, we fun ourselves in Windy Gap! Yan can easy hit wrang on t'fells.'

Food

For dinner we'd stewed geuse and haggish,
Cow'd-leady, and het bacon pie,
Nopil'd flueks, tatey-hash, beastin' puddin',
Saut salmon, and cabbish: forbye
Port, pancakes, black-puddin's, sheep trotters,

And custert, and mustert, and veal,
Grey-pez keale, and lang apple-dumplings:
I wish every yan far'd as weel.

Robert Anderson, The Coldbeck Wedding.

As much food as possible was reared or grown on the home acres. Harry Chapman, of the Youth Hostels' Association, told me of chatting with a West Cumberland farmer in the doorway of his wash-house while, inside, the farmer's son was cleaving down the middle of a suspended, newly-butchered pig.

To Harry, it seemed a neat job. The lad's father thought otherwise and remarked: 'Hod on Jonty, hod on! Thou's gaan to git baith lugs on yan side!'

A Cumbrian worker develops a healthy appetite which is not easily satisfied. When the odd-job man had finished his work, the lady who had employed him said: 'Thoo'll be riddy for thee tea. Can ta eat a boiled egg?' Said he: 'Ah yance kent a feller at eat twea [two] an' he's wick [alive] yit.' Yet another declared: 'Aye, lass—and I could eat t'ruddy hen as well.'

A group of hungry lads visited a cafe in Hawkshead early this century. The proprietress served large pancakes first, then tapered off with small ones. One lad kept saying: 'Just anudder an' then...' He was given more and continued to say: 'Just anudder an' then...' Said the proprietress: 'Anudder and then what?' He replied: 'Then start all ower agean wid them big 'uns.'

Having subsisted on home food for years, it was a treat to go elsewhere and taste other people's grub. Two farmers from the top end of Eskdale were in Barrow-in-Furness for the first time when they saw a fish and chip shop. Having heard of this delicacy, they bought some. 'Hey, Jack,' said one man after a short silence. 'These chips taste just like 'taties.'

Normally, a Cumbrian family is hospitable. 'Coom in, lad, an' hev a cup o' tea' turns out to be a full meal, with apologies there's nowt warm'—'cept tea, that is. At one farmhouse, a visitor was not offered a place at the table.

He confronted the family and told the sad tale of the sow which had thirteen lile pigs but nobbut twelve teats. When someone asked what the odd piglet did for drink, the visitor said: 'It licks it chops an' leeaks on—like I'se dewin'!'

A quarryman went shopping on behalf of his wife. At the grocer's, he asked for 'a pound o' butter, four ounce o' tea, four ounce o' yeast an' a stoan o' flour.' When the price of flour was mentioned, he protested, saying: 'Nay, I'll eat dry bread afore I pay that sooart o' money for flour.'

The schoolmistress in Borrowdale, anxious to teach the children to be thankful for blessings received, asked if any of their families regularly said grace before meals. No-one replied. She asked Lile Fred what his father said before tea. The lad replied: 'He usually says we mun go steady on t'butter.'

Funerals

The new Vicar and Sexton were not talking to each other—much. At a funeral, the animosity became apparent to all. The Vicar picked up some earth to drop into the grave. The Sexton, indignant, said: 'Now then, let's git it straight—who throw's t'muck: thee or me?'

The Carlisle Methodist wanted to be buried just inside the cemetery gates so that he would be 'first out on t'day o' Resurrection.'

A Westmorland man resigned as grave-digger on moving to another parish. His new home stood ten miles from the last. A few weeks later, he was seen digging laboriously in the churchyard, his bike propped against a wall. He told an inquirer: 'Vicar tells me they can't git anybody to take on t'job o' grave-digging. I can't leave 'em liggin' on t'top, can I?'

Golf

Two golfers found an old lady seated in the middle of the fairway at Windermere Club. 'It's dangerous for you to sit there, madam,' said one golfer. The lady beamed at them and said: 'It's all right. I'm sitting on a newspaper.'

Hardship

Times were hard. An Eskdale farmer offered to visit a friend and talk about how to live economically. They settled before the fire. The visitor blew out the candle and said: 'For a start, we don't want·any candle-leet to talk...'

Two men were chatting at Cleator Moor during the 1930s slump. One said that 'ah'm on mi feet now.' The other was about to say he was delighted when his friend held up one of his shoes. There wasn't much of the sole left.

Hounds

They are, of course, hounds—not dogs!

A man inquired from the organiser of a hound trail how far the hounds would go. 'About ten miles,' was the reply. 'Oh,' was the reply, 'I'm afraid I'm not going to follow them that far.'

The old man and his son scanned the heights of Black Combe for a sighting of a pack of hounds. The son said: 'Sither—theer's t'hoonds.' Father remarked: 'It's nobbut snaw.' Said the lad: 'Thoo's nivver sin snaw shift as fast.'

Wilf Nicholson recalled an Ambleside Sports day when an old man asked him: 'Where's the finish of the hound trail?' Wilf pointed it out. 'Not a bit o' good,' said the visitor. 'You don't want a downhill finish young man.' Wilf invited him to find some flat land. The visitor said: 'I suppose you've been given so much land in Lakeland, you've had to pile it up in great heaps.'

Industry

At Barrow, a trainee was asked if he could work with mike (micrometer) and Vernier (a kind of scale). He replied: 'I'll wark wi' anybody who's sociable.'

At Kendal, the manufacturer was asked: 'And how many people work at your place?' The manufacturer sighed and replied: 'I reckon it's about half of 'em.'

Lakes

The native, out to impress some Americans, said airily: 'That lake's bottomless. . . and if you come over here, there's one even deeper.'

Two holidaymakers hired a boat on Windermere; they fished all day and, when only an hour of daylight remained, found themselves hauling in perch by the dozen. Back on shore, one said: 'I hope you marked the spot where we caught all those fish.' 'Aye—I put a cross on t'bottom of t'boat.' The first man said: 'Nay—we might not get that boat tomorrow.'

A Bowness man bet a friend ten shillings that he could throw him across Windermere. The bet was accepted. At the first try, the man was thrown about three feet from shore. He returned to ask for his ten shillings. 'Not yet,' was the reply. 'I'll get thee across Windermere lake if it taks me aw week.'

Marriage

It surprised everyone when the Ullswater-side farmer got married—at an advanced age. 'Nay,' he explained, 'I thought I'd like to have someone to close my eyes at the end.' His friend said:

'Close your eyes? Marriage oppened mine!'

A young farmer, just married, irritated his new wife by constantly reminding her of what had happened in the house in his mother's time. No matter which household task she began, he was sure to say: 'Mudder didn't dae it that way.'

Churning morning came along. The wife filled the churn with the week's accumulation of cream, put the churn on the flags outside the back door and prepared to make butter.

Said her husband: 'Mudder didn't dae it that way.' The wife, exasperated, pulled the bung from the churn. The cream ran down the yard. She remarked: 'Did thee mudder ivver dae that?'

Medicine

If anyone was poorly, all was well if the doctor prescribed 'summat out of a bottle.' The wife of a Windermere boatman of years ago was asked by the doctor, who was re-visiting the patient: 'Does he take his medicine religiously?' 'Nay,' was the reply, 'he swears everytime I give him some.'

A man lost his wife. A friend sorrowfully asked what she had died of and was told: 'Yan o' them rare illnesses where thoo doesn't knaw thoo's gone till it's happened.'

The Keswick farmer was disappointed when the doctor charged him 7s.6d for medical attention. 'Nay,' he protested, 't'vet charged me more na that when t'oald sow were poorly.'

A neighbour asked an ailing man about his health. 'Hoo deuhs ta feel noo, lad?' he remarked. The sufferer said: 'Ah poorly. Doctor doesn't give me no hope either way.'

At Keswick, on market day, a quack-doctor was offering a pick-me-up, supplied in liquid form. He said it worked wonders. He had been using it for years. If anyone cared to squeeze a lemon, he would either get yet more droplets of juice from it or would pay the contestant £2.

The only taker was a small chap so thin the next wind might blow him over. He picked up the lemon and squeezed. For a time nothing happened. The veins on his forehead tied themselves in knots. He seemed to rock on his wasted legs. Then drops of lemon juice began to flow.

'That's remarkable,' said the quack-doctor, who was not able to get another drop from it. 'How do you account for what you've just done?' The little man said: 'I'm a church treasurer.'

Merry Neet

One 'smashing' affair described by Mrs A Wheeler, last century, included the lines:

> The fiddle was brokken to splinters,
> The window went oot wid a smash;
> The glass was a' brokken to pieces,
> Theer wasn't a yell pane i' the sash.

Motoring

When cars were uncommon, the chairman of the Bench asked a Westmerian what sort of car had caused the accident. He did not know but, trying to be helpful, added: 'It was one o' them pip-pippin sooart.'

A farmer from Stonethwaite, driving home from Keswick, had a terrible feeling he had forgotten something. The feeling lasted until he arrived home and remembered. It was his wife.

Old Age

Forty years ago, I asked a somewhat testy Coniston man how old he was and he replied: 'Eighty-four'. Thinking I would compliment him, I said: 'You don't look eighty-four.' He snapped back: 'Can't help that!'

That same day, an old man at Penruddock, near Penrith, when asked how he felt, said: 'Not so weal. I'se yan foot in t'grave and yan on a banana skin, ready for slippin' in.'

An inclination towards grumbling comes to many as the years roll by. A man who was persuaded to peel potatoes found himself scraping away earth as well as the jackets, and observed: 'If we gang on like this, there'll be no farms left.'

A somewhat mean Langsleddale farmer listened while his farm man told him that years had passed since he had given him a rise in his wage. 'I'd be ashamed if my friends got to knaw hoo little thoo's payin' me.' The farmer said: 'Dooan't fret, lad. I won't tell anybody.

An East Fellside (Edenvale) farmer kept his son poor and when he died there was nothing for the lad, who lamented: ''E telt me nowt! 'E left me nowt! Come to think of it—he said I wor good for nowt!'

Owls

A Methodist minister in Westmorland, returning from a late call, heard a terrible screech and, thinking someone was in pain, entered the nearest house to inquire. As the householder opened the door, another screech was sounded. 'Nay,' she said to the minister, 'it's nobbit a hullett [owl].'

A Leeds man was camping in Langdale. He was chatting to a local farmer as a weird sound was heard. 'What was that?' asked the visitor, to be told it was an owl. 'I know that,' he persisted, 'but what was 'owling?'

Royalty

At a Kendal school, a boy was asked what God does. He replied: 'He saves our gracious Queen.'

Princes Louise was one of the Royals who visited Lakeland. The present Queen and members of her family have been here, too, and she had tea at one of the National Trust farmsteads near Coniston.

A former Prince of Wales, aged about sixteen, visited Grasmere with his friend, young Lord Cadogan. They rowed out to the island in the lake and, being high spirited, began to chase the sheep.

An old woman who owned the sheep shouted to the young men that they should leave the sheep alone. They ignored her. She began to scold them, using far-from-polite words.

When someone told her she had been telling off the Prince of Wales and a Lord, the old lady replied: 'Aa care nowt whae they are. They're badly browt-up bairns, an' they'd dew wi' t'brakkin-strap puttin' on a bit. . .'

The large hotel near the lake is named—*Prince of Wales!*

Salesmanship

Frank Robinson, who owned the fent shop on Cragg Brow, Bowness, was a man of sharp and original thought. His motto was 'poor but honest—nobbut just.'

His stated resolution was expressed as follows: 'For the past 43 years I have been diddling the public right and left, and have never been locked up yet. For the next 75 years I intend reversing the process, and hope for the best.'

Frank's attitude to humour was 'Folk et can't laff et owt that's really funny, owt ta see a dockter.' A very witty person, he once remarked: 'Any shirt is better than no shirt. But our shirts are better than any shirts. One customer told us he had only one fault to find with them. He had worn one six weeks and it wanted washing.'

Schooldays

Many are the tales told out of school of things that happened in school. A teacher, having gone through the Beatitudes to a class at Ulverston, said: 'Blessed are they that mourn. What is it to mourn?' The reply from a small girl was: 'Saturday.'

The Sawrey schoolmistress asked a class where one finds elephants. A lad replied: 'An elephant's such a girt animal it doesn't git lost.'

At Milnthorpe school, the Kent estuary was described picturesquely by a small girl as 'a river with its mouth full of mud.'

Sport

Footballers start young. A lad in a West Cumberland town, while playing football, damaged (more precisely, shattered!) a window and was collared by a policemen who thought he would scare him by taking him towards the police station.

A number of his friends stood at the street corner as he passed. The lad, determined to keep a stiff upper lip, was taunted by one lad who said: 'What's happened?'

'Nay,' was the reply. 'They've just asked me to play for t'police.'

A Whitehaven footballer broke a bone in his hand but carried on playing as though nothing had happened. Another member of the team queried his attitude. He replied: 'Nay, I'd rather put up wi' t'pain than tell t'wife. If I ever complain about something, she tells me to stop smoking.'

Transport

In the days when horses were masters of the dusty road, a Kendal lad asked a local farmer how much it would cost to hire one. The farmer first wanted to know the duration of the loan. 'How long do you want a hoss?' he inquired. The lad replied: 'As long as thoo's got; there's five on us.'

The rider of a penny farthing seen descending Dunmail Raise with his legs resting on the handlebars later explained the bike had 'uptipped' so often on the rough road, next time he was determined to land on his feet rather than his nose.

Alexander Pearson, in *The Doings of a Country Solicitor,* recalled having difficulty in starting his car. A local lady asked what was the matter, and added: 'Is the engine causing trouble?' Pearson replied: 'Yes, it's the engine misbehaving. But there's nothing surprising in that, for I always expect to get trouble from anything under a bonnet.'

Between Grasmere and Ambleside, the bus was full and two old ladies were having to stand. A hefty man turned to a schoolboy on the front seat and remarked: 'Hesn't thoo any manners? Why doesn't thoo git on thee legs and let yan o' these ladies hev thee seat?' The boy replied: 'Stand up theesel. Then there'd be room for beath o' them to sit doon.'

A motor coach from the Midlands disgorged its passengers at Shap for 'toilets and tea'. At a local cafe, the friendly proprietor asked a man if he had been in the village before. He shook his head. The shopkeeper remarked: 'Shap's like a piece of elastic—it stretches.'

Wartime

Visitors to Lakeland in the 1939-45 war were astonished to find plenty of good farm food at a time when they were having to manage on their sparse rations.

A farmer who was shifting some 'black market' meat in his little old van was waved down by the police. His wife said to him: 'Thoo's hed it this time. They'll cop you.'

The farmer 'put his foot down' and passed the policemen at high speed. His fretful wife said: 'They'll have got your car number.' He said: 'Doan't worry. I plastered it wi' cow muck afore we set off.'

The Home Guard was originally the Local Defence Volunteers, LDV for short. The initials were said to mean: 'Look, Duck and Vanish'. The force attracted men of all shapes, sizes, ages and degrees of comprehension. On one parade, the men were told to move two paces forward. All did this—except a man who remarked to the sergeant: 'It'd save a lot o' trouble if thoo'd move two paces ehint [back].'

Weather

Oh Wasdale, where are thy charms,
That poets have found in thy face;
Better dwell in the midst of alarms,
Than stay in this watery place.

From a Visitors' book of Wasdale Head (1869).

Someone observed: 'Not one day in a Lake-week deserves the name of Sunday.' Crabb Robinson wrote to William Wordsworth: 'Did I once see a bright sun in Cumberland or Westmorland?'

The weather is variable and the seasons tend to git mixed up. A farmer near Kendal was heard to say: 'Ah heard someone tell 'at winter's on t'way. I don't believe 'em. They said t'same thing about summer.'

There is a modest pride in the severity of the Lakeland weather. A farmer said to a tourist who was complaining about the rain: 'Wet? You don't call this wet. You can say it's raining if ducks decide to go into t'hoose.'

The weather is a good talking point. Two Ambleside men who were trying to forecast conditions over the next day or two had a splendid view of the snow-whitened slopes of Fairfield and its neighbours. One man remarked: 'T'weather won't git warmer till t'snaw's off yon mountains.' His companion replied: 'An' t'snaw won't gang off t'mountains till it gits warmer.'

Wordsworth

It is said that when news that William Wordsworth had died spread through the district, an old Grasmere resident said he was very sorry to hear it. Then, brightening, he added: 'But niver mind. T'mistress is a cliverish kind o' body. I reckon she'll carry on t'business.'

Will Ritson, of Wasdale, said of Wordsworth: 'He wor a varra quiet aad men. He'd nea pride aboot him an' varra lile to say.'

Spoken Like a Cumbrian...

OF MARRIAGE: (1) 'Nivver thee wed a woman wid a fortune. My wife hed five pund, an' I nivver heard t'last on't.' (2) 'Fwolks talks about love! Wey, issent it just as easy to love a lass wid a lot o' brass as yan et has none?'

Of the east wind: 'It's too lazy to blaw roound thee—it gaes straight through!'

Of a slow-going son: 'Our Frank's just like a cow tail—he's allus ahint.'

Of a rogue: 'Crooked bi nature is nivver med straight bi eddication.'

Of a troubled man: 'He snwores at yah end an' belches winnd at t'udder.'

Some Radio Talks

Wellies and Binder Twine

There must have been Life in Rural Cumbria before the introduction of Wellies and Binder Twine—but that Life cannot have amounted to much.

This thought was prompted by a visit to Dentdale, during which I saw:

(a) a farmer wearing wellies, one black and one green;

(b) a genuine Dentdale 'welly gate' and its rare variant, namely the Dunlop gate;

(c) ten miles of binder twine being used in all sorts of ingenious ways, from keeping field gates together to holding up a farmer's trousers.

The Cumbrian farmer was, indeed, a pioneer of re-cycling.

I had crossed from Kingsdale into Deepdale—on a high highway. It was mountaineering on four wheels. This time, the wheels had to cope with snow and ice.

The upper dale resounded with the bleating of sheep. A shepherd who overtook me was not of the Old English type, wearing a smock and carrying a crook, in the manner of Thomas Hardy's shepherd.

This northern shepherd was a young man on a Japanese motortrike—an adult toy: the sort of machine which has made farming fun. A light-alloy crook lay on the trike. The shepherd's faithful dog, which was sitting on the pillion seat, managed to maintain its equilibrium without the help of a seat belt. Somehow, room had been found for a bale or two of hay.

It was one of those days when RAF jets were putting a bit of life into the languid air. A fell farmer—exaggerating a little—said he'd seen t'draught from an airyplane 'bowl ower' some of his sheep. 'Aye—an' t'dog had to hang on or it would hev bin blawn away.'

Now let me remind you of point (a)—about the farmer who wore a black welly and a green welly. He'd been brought up in the days of 'waste not, want not'. On the first occasion I saw this sort of economy, and thought it was most unusual, the farmer said: 'Nowt o' t'sooart. My lad's getten a pair just like it!'

Now to point (b)—that Welly Gate. You may have seen one attached to an old-fashioned stile in a wall. It's a small gate, designed not so much to restrict walkers as to deter footloose sheep, which otherwise would squeeze through the gap from one field to another.

It depends for its effectiveness on the soles of redundant wellies—soles which are cut away and used as hinges. You apply pressure to the gate to open it. The gate closes behind you with a decisive clunk!

These gates have been a feature of Dentdale for years and are now to be found all over Lakeland and the Pennines. It's too good an idea to be wasted. The Dunlop Gate is one of similar size and purpose but, instead of using welly soles, the farmer has cut bits from an old motor tyre. It also has the strength and elasticity to keep a stile gate tightly shut.

As for point (c)—binder twine—this is the stuff purchased for use with field-baled hay. You will have seen a tractor and baling machine clonking across a field with the hay being packed tightly, wrapped with twine and jettisoned as bales which are usually just too heavy for comfortable handling. (This harks back to the time when there was a lot of contract-baling. The farmer, paying so much a bale, wanted his money's worth).

It is important to account for every bit of twine in case the farm stock eats some with the hay. So every farm has its abundance of binder twine. I have seen a Lakeland farmer with a foot in plaster, hobbling across a yard with the plaster swaddled in a plastic fertiliser sack bound with twine—his way of keeping the plaster clean.

I have seen binder twine used to hold up trousers, to fettle up a gate and to restrain a lively dog.

Now we're in the age of 'Big Bale Silage'. The grass is taken green, baled and slipped into a big plastic bag to exclude the air. In a wet summer, each bag may also hold a gallon or two of water.

This silage looks repulsive, but the cattle enjoy it. And that, as they say, is the object of the game.

Parson and Kirk

I asked a Lakeland parson about his parish routine. Mention was made of his 'flock'. He smiled and cracked a parsonic joke: 'There are white sheep on the hill and black sheep in the valley.'

Another clerk, who has a dwindling as well as ageing congregation, said: 'The young people are missing. Half the folk I preach to could drop dead tomorrow.' It was not morbidity but a simple statement of fact.

In Victorian days, parsons ranked next to the principal landowner in the Lakeland social set-up. They might give the impression of being busy but had time, means and leisure. Today's clergymen have to run to keep up with their multi-parish responsibilities. In the study is such electronic wizardry as an answerphone and word-processor. The vicar has developed a twitch.

The Victorians built some splendid churches in the Lake District proper. One of the most imposing, St Mary's at Ambleside, has a spire which tickles the clouds.

Happily, there still remain—tucked away from the sight of the modern world—the tiny meeting places for worship. These are

59

most evocative of the old Lakeland way of life. Some of the parsons who attended them had 'whittlegate', which meant they could take their cutlery along to the home of a parishioner for their meals.

The old chapel of Wasdale Head crouches so low it is almost hidden by a cluster of yew trees. In 1845, it had neither enclosing fence nor doors. A thorn bush jammed into the entrance kept out nomadic sheep. The building was bedded with bracken, like a stable. There were only two pews, the other seats being trestles, held up by sheep-forms.

One service ended abruptly when the pulpit collapsed. The vicar found himself on the lap of a woman who sat in the front pew.

Old-time parsons were as characterful as the buildings in which they preached. Mr Sewell of Wythburn lost his notes down a crack beside the pulpit. The sermon was lost but he promptly offered to read 'a chapter of the Bible worth ten of it.'

Consider Richard Birkett, the parson at Martindale for 67 years. When he arrived in this remote valley near Ullswater, he had two shirts and a suit of clothes. He drew less than £3 a year from the church and had to take on other jobs. He married a woman who had £60. When Birkett died, she could put her hands on £1,200.

In Birkett's time, Easter dues were paid in eggs. The farmers were soon made to realise that they could not dispose of small eggs by giving them to the parson. Birkett used a special gauge, which was simply a board in which a hole had been cut. If an egg passed through the hole, it was handed back to the farmer who had brought it. A larger egg was demanded.

Owd Sarah Yewdale, who was called Queen of Borrowdale, recalled when folk went to church on horseback. On wedding days, nearly everyone and every horse was be-ribboned, though 'some stole off as they do now to get wedded, and never a dog barked. Nobody was wiser until it was all over.'

Folk generally made 'a great do' of weddings. There'd be as many as twenty or thirty go to the kirk on nag's back...It was a very cheerful sight to see them all going down the road in a long string on a fine morning.'

A Cumbrian who has got beyond the Biblical span of three score years, asked about his health as he hobbled out of the kirk, replied: 'I reckon t'burner's gone oot, but t'pilot light's still in.'

Who has not heard of Wonderful (Robert) Walker? He was born in the Duddon Valley in 1709, being the youngest and weakest of a large family. There was nowt for it but to have him 'bred a scholar'. He became a schoolteacher at Buttermere, married a lass who had a dowry of £40 ('the principal of which was never touched') and eventually settled down as parson and schoolmaster at Seathwaite, in his native valley. This 'wreckling' of the family died in 1802, aged 93.

He and his family developed the noble North Country art of living off next to nowt. Wordsworth, no mean hand at simple living, found that Walker had but one luxury—a woollen covering to his family pew, spun by Walker's own hands. Wordsworth mentioned Walker's clerical activities, often carried out at night. Walker spent his daytime hours teaching, gardening, attending to a few cows and sheep on the fellside, cultivating several fields, and much else. Here were no idle hands for the Devil to make use of!

As curate, he received £5 a year when he arrived and never drew more than £50 during his long spell of service. He spent liberally only on the welfare of his children. His (frugal) wife died a few months before him. They left £2,000—for the family to spend.

Lonsdale Yellow

I was once mistaken for Lord Lonsdale—not the present holder of that title but one of his ancestors, Hugh, the 5th Earl. This flamboyant, cigar-smoking character of the late Victorian and

Edwardian periods was nicknamed The Yellow Earl.

Some say it was because of the light tone of his hair. Others claim it followed his passion for painting his carriages yellow (which was also the colour adopted by the Conservative Party in Old Westmorland).

How was it possible for me—a very ordinary sort of person, driving a Ford Escort—to be taken for the man who was a friend of Royalty and who lived in great splendour at Lowther Park, near Penrith?

It was all a matter of colour, more precisely that canary-yellow.

I'd driven up Martindale, the secluded valley lying east of Ullswater. At Dale Head, the farmer looked at my yellow car and said: 'By gow, lad, but I thought Owd Lordy was comin' back to see us.'

Lordy, renting the deer-stalking in Martindale, let everyone know he was around. He and his friends arrived in yellow-painted carriages or cars. They stayed at a lodge of Austrian style which may still be seen perched on the hillside, overlooking the Nab, which is the centrepiece of the Martindale deer forest.

Lordy's partiality for yellow led to a story that Lonsdale yellow was selected as the colour for vehicles owned by the Automobile Association. It is a good story, but unsubstantiated, though Lordy was the first president of the AA.

John Peel, a descendant of the huntsman, rose in the service of the Lowthers to become chief accountant. In his retirement, I sometimes called to see him at his 17th century home at Lowther Newtown. (This 'new town' was established in 1680).

John's father worked on the Lowther Estate. Each day he went shopping in Penrith, using a heavy horse-drawn van—painted yellow, of course—until, in the 1920s, it was succeeded by a motor van, which was also yellow.

I heard from John Peel of the splendour at Lowther Castle, now simply a facade looming beyond the greensward of Lowther Park, which is crossed by a public road. Lordy extended his parkland by flattening farms and hedges until it exceeded in size that of the Howards of Greystoke. He made Lowther the largest private park in England.

What was he really like—Hugh Cecil, 5th Earl of Lonsdale, who was known, but never to his face, as the Yellow Earl? John Peel described him to me as 'a fine, big, healthy-looking man, full of life and vigour. You knew immediately that he was someone special. He was not the first head of the family to have his carriages painted yellow. His nickname must have been derived from his sandy-coloured hair.'

Lordy lived at a good time—for people who had brass. Taxes were low. In rural areas, he could draw on a reserve of cheap, respectful labour. And it was a time when country houses, unlike medieval castles, could be comfortable.

John Peel used the back door of the castle when he met Lordy by appointment. At the entrance to the Earl's study were two stuffed huskies, souvenirs of a trip to the Arctic. Animal rugs lay on the floor. Representations of snakes were attached to trellis work. The Earl sat at a large desk. John Peel perched on the edge of the padded leather of a huge chair.

I enjoyed hearing tales about him. It was a special pleasure when, many years ago, I drove up to Dale Head Farm, in Martindale, to hear the farmer say—with reference to my canary-yellow car: 'By gow, lad, but I thowt Owd Lordy was coming back to see us.'

Old Time Traffic

Very early one morning, I was intercepted by the police while motoring on the M6 just south of Shap. They wanted to know who owned my car. 'And, sir, do you mind telling us where you are going?'

The first part was not too difficult. I had some documentary evidence about ownership. I wasn't sure what the police reaction would be to the second point. I remarked, lamely, 'I'm going to see the sun rise over Haweswater.'

Fortunately, they believed me—or I would have been late for an appointment with Nature.

The notion of travelling in heated comfort over Shap Fell at 70 miles an hour, using a multi-lane road on which I could over-take traffic at will, would have seemed fantastic when I took up motoring and directed my first small car along the old A6.

It was a two-tone car—all black paint and rust. It suffered from tappet rattle, piston slap and goodness knows what else. It had to be coaxed. Consequently, I hoped that on the gruelling climb from Kendal to Shap I wouldn't get stuck behind a Pickford's van or a cattle wagon.

The first time I drove through the Wilderness of Shap to the Promised Land of the Eden Valley, I was so elated I gave the car its head. It rattled in protest as the speedometer needle flickered at a most daring 50 miles an hour. I held it at that speed for a minute or two before easing my foot from the accelerator. I had visions of the mudguards falling off.

A friend replaced some rotten floorboards with what I thought was good wood. It turned out to be a composition board. After several soakings in water thrown up from the puddly roads, the flooring let me down.

As I drove in Borrowdale, I had a sinking feeling. Looking down, I saw a gap, below which—clearly visible—was the road. I shifted my weight a little and coaxed the car to a joiner's shop in Keswick. The joiner—bless him—provided me with floorboards (the sort used in a house) and creosoted them while I waited.

Jonty Wilson, one-time blacksmith at Kirkby Lonsdale, was fond of yarning about the Galloway Gate, 130 miles long, extending from lowland Lancashire through Cumbria to south-west Scotland.

Now the Galloway Gate (said Jonty) was a forerunner of the M6. I heard of the sturdy trains of pack-horses which used it. Jonty respected 't'owd Gallowa', as he called the stocky animal.

After chatting with Jonty, who had in turn chatted with a pack-horse owner (his Grandfather), I could picture the packman, striding along, wearing hodden grey coat, knee breeches, woollen stockings and a low-crowned beaver hat (made of rabbit skins). Many packmen had clogs on their feet.

The Galloway Gate began to lose its importance about 1860. Better roads and, in due course, the railway hastened its decline. The old inns reverted to being just farms.

Jonty had heard that at one inn, 'mine host' looked out of a window at the leaden sky and said to a packman: 'It looks like rain.' 'Aye,' was the reply from the packman, after he had glanced at the ale he had bought: 'And it tastes like it as well.'

Fireside Christmas

Fire provided warmth and comfort to our remote Cumbrian ancestors. It has been replaced in many homes by electric or gas fires.

The last time I met Norman Nicholson, the Cumbrian poet, was at his Millom fireside on a chill December afternoon when neither of us felt like wandering far. I commented on the fireplace, with its handsome marble surround. Norman remarked: 'It's not marble; it's painted slate.'

Lady Anne Clifford, when visiting her Westmorland castles in the seventeenth century, toasted herself beside a fire made of Tan Hill coal. She enjoyed fireside comforts in preference to a hot bath. She recommended her friends to have one bath a year, whether or not it was necessary.

A pre-Christmas treat was to call on Tissie Fooks, of Hay Bridge near Bouth, and sip coffee before a fire of logs, which spluttered and hissed, projecting large sparks into the room.

Tissie had established a nature reserve in the Rusland Valley and for seven years I served on the committee. One snowtime, when a meeting was held at Low Hay Bridge, I completed the last part of the journey on snow and ice and then enjoyed all the old wintertime features—a crackling fire, in setting of grey stonework; rich fellowship and a bowl of roe deer soup.

Tissie died in February, two days before her 87th birthday. Just before Christmas, on impulse, I called to see her at High Hay Bridge, a converted barn. It was at the close of day—known to countryfolk as 't'edge o' dark'.

The room, faintly illuminated by lights in heavy shades and by fingers of orange light from the fire, looked as mysterious and as fascinating as ever. I sat beside a log fire, feeling the warmth seeping into my bones.

I was under the beady gaze of a stuffed moose head, one of her late husband's sporting trophies, which was fixed on the wall above the fireplace. Out of the corner of one eye, I saw the gleam in the eye of a tiger—a glass eye, set in a beast which happily was represented only by its head and skin.

As I prepared to leave Hay Bridge, with an exchange of Christmas greetings, I fixed in my mind the comforting image of a fire made of wood. I'm sure that the stuffed moose, warmed by the upflow of air from the fire, winked at me!

Night Shift on Helvellyn

Does the sun ever shine on Helvellyn? Whenever I scramble to the top, I encounter Lakeland mist, which you can taste and—between the hours of 8.30 am and 9.30 am—may have a fried bacon flavour, wafted up from the Glenridding guest houses.

Bob assures me that Helvellyn does occasionally have the sun's rays upon it. The last time we discussed the matter, he became more eloquent by the minute as he outlined plans for a major operation to climb the fell.

We would reach a point just before the Hole in the Wall, on the way to Striding Edge, and watch the summer sun rise like a fireball from behind Cross Fell.

How could Colin and I refuse the chance to accompany him on a pre-dawn sortie to a Lakeland giant? There would be the prospect of seeing 'for ten minutes at least' the Ullswater district, its lakes and mountains, all tinted ruby-red.

Bob said that on a summer sunrise, Red Tarn, which is normally a cheerless, shadowy area, truly lives up to its name, with a redness like blood. The experience of being on the 'tops' at sunrise would live with us till the end of our days.

We met, in stockinged feet, in the kitchen of his home for a pre-expedition 'brew'. I sipped meditatively, thinking of another Moonlighter expedition he organised. This was to High Street, to see a red Haweswater, red sheep and (hopefully) some red red deer.

As related, the Cumbrian constabulary stopped us on the M6. We were asked where we were going. I gulped and replied, lamely, hardly expecting to be believed: 'To see the sunrise.'

If the two young policemen thought we were made to do this for pleasure, they did not allow their facial muscles to convey this idea.

At dawn, on that trip to Haweswater, we looked from our ridge approach to High Street on to a bank of cloud. Bob muttered something about the law of averages and said we must try again.

So now three of us motored through noctural Lakeland on our way to Helvellyn. We passed through villages where the only sign of life was the occasional bedroom light burning and the moggies on patrol.

Bob adroitly steered his car so that it would not flatten a jay-walking hedgehog. By lucky chance, he also missed the migrating toad.

Bob said: 'I always think that when I've done a Moonlighter, I've gained a day...Of course, I've got to hand that day back again when I collapse with fatigue twenty-four hours later.'

At Glenridding, he produced one of those large battery-operated lights devised for motorists in distress. We would need some artificial light on the first stage of the walk, he said, adding that the battery would 'go flat' in less than an hour. This last tit-bit of information added wings to our feet.

The air in the Glenridding valley had all the stuffiness of a tropical night. We began to walk from the car at 2.45, disturbing the snooze pattern of sheep and lambs which had settled on the broad white path for their eight hours of sleep. This would be followed by eight hours of grazing and eight hours of chewing the cud. I suddenly felt sorry for sheep.

We passed Lanty's Tarn, surrounded by trees which in the gloom seemed as insubstantial as shadows. The hinges of the swing gates were squeaky, providing a variation on the Dawn Chorus. As light began to spread across the sky in a pearl-grey wash, a blackbird in Grizedale Valley tuned up for its part in the aforementioned chorus.

The electric lamp which had illuminated our path became redundant as we settled down for the Long Drag to the Hole in the Wall, which presaged Striding Edge and Helvellyn. Chirpy meadow pipits brought a semblance of life to the tousled vegetation beside the path.

A mini-drought of several weeks duration ended. The Weather Clerk summoned a stiff breeze from the south-west; a curtain of cloud was drawn across the sky and large droplets of rain fell on to a grateful earth.

[A few hours before, I read an item from the 150 years ago feature of *The Westmorland Gazette* about a Victorian drought which had shrivelled up the fields and caused anxiety to Lakeland farmers].

The path from Glenridding carried us up for some 1,800 feet, into a realm of outcrops composed of slabs which held each other vertically in ancient vices. From the misty crags came the 'kronking' of ravens, doubtless a family party of birds.

We sat—three of us—waiting for the 'fireball' effect which would transform the greys and blues of the landscape into vivid reds. We looked eastwards until our eyes prickled with fatigue, but there was nowt but cloud and mist.

So we contented ourselves by studying the pin-pricks of light which indicated the position of Penrith. In due course, the Pennines—Defoe's 'wall of brass'—came faintly into view.

Bob said: 'There's just a vague redness in the sky.' Colin thought it was really a 'mucky brown'. To me it was plain, old-fashioned grey. . .

We breakfasted at an elevation which, in Bob's picturesque speech, was 'kissing 3,000 feet'. Some excitement had been provided by Striding Edge, the half mile long shattered ridge where the most venturesome of the paths extended along the top of dramatic undulations, with upjutting rock under the feet and dizzying views on either side.

Having crossed the rim of Helvellyn, we paid homage at the memorial plaque to Charles Gough, who died from a fall and whose remains were guarded by his faithful dog for three months.

The summit of Helvellyn on this misty day was a place to vacate at the earliest opportunity. Bob recalled days when everything was plated with snow and ice.

As we turned valleywards, the sky cleared. It was 8.30 am— bacon-frying time in the hotels and guest houses. After the frustration of mist and cloud, patches of blue sky appeared to view.

The first of the diurnal visitors to Helvellyn, trudging up the path, smiled and remarked: 'I think this is going to be a lovely sunny day.'

Venison for Dinner

Rudolph, the red-nosed reindeer, who has his praises sung during Christmas, is unusual in having a 'very shiny nose'. Every other reindeer has a nose which is covered with fine hair, a form of protection in a cold climate.

Reindeer, with or without shiny noses, have not been seen in Lakeland for several thousand years, except as illustrations on modern Christmas cards. The species was unsuited to the warmer conditions following the melting of the glacial ice.

Some reindeer lingered in northern Scotland until the twelfth century. Reindeer from another part of the northern world were re-introduced, to the Cairngorms, in modern times.

Red deer were emparked by the high and mighty families of Lakeland. Deer park, dovecote and fish-pond were not just to beautify an estate; in the days before refrigerators, they represented to my lord and his family a source of fresh protein in the midst of winter.

The peasants of Cumbria, subsisting on a few dry rations, must have spent many a restless winter night dreaming about sinking their teeth into gobbets of venison.

In Wet Sleddale are the impressive remains of a large deer trap. On an appointed day, men drove the deer from the fells into the dale and the luckless animals converged on the trap—an enclosure, with high walls. An ingenious baffle led the deer into captivity and here they were retained and fed until my lord's pantry was in need of fresh supplies.

In 1660, Daniel Fleming, as Sheriff of Cumberland, entertained the Judges on Assize to a rib-stretching meal which included venison from red deer which had roamed Ennerdale and Martindale. Ennerdale yielded 'as great Hartts and Staggs as in any part of England'.

Will you be tucking into venison this Christmas? My lord's deer park has become the entrepreneur's deer-farm. And, for most families, turkey will be carved on Christmas Day.

The turkey was introduced into England from North America. Our medieval Cumbrian lord would never have heard of it.

Happy New Year

An account of New Year's Eve festivities at a Westmorland farmhouse appears in Mr Rumney's book entitled *The Dalesman*, published by Titus Wilson of Kendal in 1911.

In those days, the party spirit was generated through homemade fun—feasting and dancing—in a stone-flagged kitchen.

Today we are offered triangular sandwiches, vol-au-vents and trifle with squirted cream out of an aerosol cannister. Mr Rumney's

New Year's Eve celebrations began with real food—with plates of beef and chicken-pie. Someone served chocolates and sweetmeats. The old folk thought it was needlessly extravagant.

One of the lads who fancied himself as a fiddler had brought his instrument with him. Tables and chairs were pushed back to clear some space for dancing.

When the fiddler 'broke down'—through sheer exhaustion, I suppose—men carried on the tune by means of a paper and comb, until the fiddler recovered. We read that the men's nailed boots made a rare clatter on the flags, and there were not a few slips, with an occasional spark of fire from the nails. No one actually fell.

A shottische, a three-reel, the plain quadrilles and even the Lancers followed. Mr Jackson and Miss Thompson pressed hard for a waltz, but this was beyond the fiddler's powers, and they had to be content with John Peel, which made an excellent gallop...

The dance was about to end, at midnight, when the host, Tyson, appeared at the parlour door and shouted out a cheery: 'Happy new year to you all...'

By the time the greetings had been exchanged, the New Year was already ten minutes old.

A former vicar of Applethwaite told me when Church time stood still. The clock ceased to function. No bells were heard marking the quarter-hours.

Then someone remembered that many years before a man took on the voluntary job of clock-winder. As time went by, people forgot his generous offer.

Now the clock had stopped. Inquiries were made. It was found that the clock-winder, an unsung hero, had died...

Dancing Daffodils

The daffodils first 'danced' for Dorothy Wordsworth.

I refer to THE daffodils—the golden host which Dorothy's brother, William, saw 'beside the lake, beneath the trees, fluttering and dancing in the breeze.'

It was in April, 1802, when brother and sister beheld the daffodils while walking beside Ullswater. Dorothy confided in her journal: 'When we were in the woods beyond Gowbarrow Park we saw a few daffodils close to the waterside.'

These plants were of the small wild variety, as seen in some old tracts of woodland—near Burneside, in the Rusland Valley and elsewhere. Dorothy wrote of the Ullswater plants that '. . . they tossed and reeled and danced, and seemed as if they verily laughed with the wind.'

William Wordsworth transformed the prose into splendid verse which begins: 'I wandered lonely as a cloud'. He wasn't lonely, of course, for he was in the company of Dorothy. And, come to think of it, there is no such thing as a lonely cloud in an area like Lakeland, with its cloud-making mountains.

The poem Daffodils was a 'combined operation'. William's wife, Mary, suggested the thought which was enshrined in the lines: 'They flash upon that inward eye / Which is the bliss of solitude.'

The large, cultivated strains of daffodils have triumphed over the little wild variety. Point Nought Nought Nought One per cent of the land surface of Lakeland is now covered with daffodils.

I make a special point in late March or early April of motoring along the Golden Mile, which in this case is not at Blackpool but between the northern end of the Kendal by-pass and Crook. The roadsides are lined with cheerful daffs.

An Eden Valley friend who was associated with the Ministry of

Agriculture during the 1939-45 war told me of visits to the gardens of Lowther Castle, near Penrith, when the head gardener was Mr Jefferies. An important theme was 'Dig for Victory', and an encouragement of everyone to grow their own food, but sometimes the talk came round to flowers.

Mr Jefferies related the familiar story that Lord Lonsdale [celebrated Yellow Earl] was partial to yellow. The family coaches were painted in this colour. Botanically, he loved yellow flowers, especially daffodils.

Lord Lonsdale instructed his gardener to prolong the daffodil-flowering season as much as possible by 'bringing on' early blooms and retarding others. This was a torment to the head gardener, who was allergic to daffodil pollen.

Each spring, his poor wife spent much of her time rubbing 'gentian violet' on his body and she moaned when it stained the bed sheets, for it was not an easy matter to restore them to their gleaming whiteness.

When his Lordship died, his grave was lined with daffodils.

Miss Potter's Room

This year we are celebrating—if that is the right word—the fiftieth anniversary of the death of Beatrix Potter.

She who had a sheltered upbringing in a large Victorian house in London, and who spent some languid holidays in Lakeland before settling down at Sawrey, died in time of war, when the Lakeland sky shivered to the drone of German bombers heading for the shipyards of Barrow.

Nearly everyone in the Lake District must know by now that Beatrix married William Heelis, a solicitor. She became an enthusiastic sheep-farmer besotted by the herdwick breed. When she bequeathed to the National Trust some of the largest sheep farms, it was a condition of ownership that space should be found for Lakeland's own little breed of sheep.

By her generosity, Beatrix ensured that herdwicks still occupy the farms of central Lakeland, though a Langdale farmer says of the old Lakeland breed: 'Nowadays, it's more historic than profitable.' I thought of her as I walked up the quieter side of the Troutbeck valley, near Windermere—a valley flanked by the lean ridges of the fells that have gathered round High Street.

Into view came that curious lump of ground known as the Tongue—a squelchy area, its sides thick with bracken. In due course I was looking down on Troutbeck Park farmhouse, a substantial white-walled building which Beatrix bought in 1923 and loved to visit by chauffeur-driven car.

One of my visits, years ago, was prompted by a chat I had with Tom Storey, her old shepherd, who lived at Sawrey. In 1926, his farming employer, Noble Gregg, of Town End, Troutbeck, decided to retire and Tom was left looking for another job.

Mrs Heelis, complete with tweedy clothes and clogs, appeared at the door of the shippon where he was milking cows. She asked his name. Tom told her.

She said: 'Will you come and work for me at Troutbeck Park?' Tom said that he didn't mind—if the money was right!

'How old are you?' asked Mrs Heelis. 'I'm thirty,' Tom replied, whereupon she declared: 'Oh—I'm sixty.' She promptly announced that if Tom would work for her, she would double his existing wage. He began at Troutbeck Park on the following Monday.

I remember, on an old-time visit to the famous farmhouse, entering a little room which Mrs Heelis maintained here for her own use. As the door swung open, I could see by the type of furnishings and their arrangement it had not been disturbed for years. On the wall was an old painting of the Troutbeck Park estate.

Anthony Benson, who first worked at the Park when he was a lad fresh from school—and who was now living in retirement in a village near Penrith—remembered the room. He also mentioned Mrs Heelis's old dog, Bob, which was 'a lile bow-legged thing', though it had been a good dog in its time.

Troutbeck Park was [according to Tom Storey] her favourite farm. 'She'd take a sandwich with her and go for a walk on to Tongue End. If I happened to be away up t'fell, she'd wait for me to come back. She carried a stick, not a crook, with her...'

I mentioned the lile room at the farmhouse, hoping to hear from Tom that she had done some of her writing here. It is unlikely.

Said Tom: 'It wasn't often she could be persuaded to go into t'farm kitchen for a drink o' tea. She just had her sandwiches, which were lapped [wrapped] in a piece of paper.'

Tom paused, then said: 'She usually ate 'em outside.'

Ferry Boat on Windermere

When things quieten down a bit, after a summer of low-flying aircraft and high-flying motor boats, I really must travel on the posh new Windermere ferry.

I'm bound to compare it with its predecessor of 40 years ago. Commissioned in 1914, that ferry had a slight list, an appetite for coal and a Woodbine-type chimney which puffled out soot as well as smoke. It provided extra trade for the Lakeland dry-cleaners.

The voyage then—as now—lasted a few minutes. I first crossed in the 1940s, when Short Brothers, who had a factory where the Lakes School now stands, sent yet another Sunderland Flying Boat into the air. It was an awesome sight, with four engines droning.

When I next used the ferry, in 1952, Jack Bowman of Windermere was still an important member of the crew and the service was being operated by the Westmorland Joint Ferry Committee. The steam engine had a daily intake of five hundredweights of coal.

Jack reminded me that for the voyage of precisely 720 yards, the ferry was kept to a precise course by two cables, stretching from a point just south of Bowness to one near what had been the Ferry Hotel. Jack showed me a letter he received from a lady living down South. She wanted to book a berth for the ferry crossing.

There was no fuss as the old Windermere ferry boat touched the shingle after its six minutes voyage. The ramp was lowered, the shingle was raked smooth and there was an exodus of passengers and what were then called motor-cars. Little did we know they would breed like rabbits and swamp the district.

John Hoggarth, of Far Sawrey, remembered when the ferry was a large rowing boat, with four men to do the rowing. If horses and carts were being transported, the horses were taken out of the shafts to conserve space.

'There were days when we never knew if we were in t'boat or in t'lake. It was nowt fresh in foggy weather for us to be two or three miles off-course. A man's only so much strength in his arms when he's in a boat. I never took much harm, though—only wet!'

Jack Bowman remembered when some cows 'abandoned ship' and swam ashore, where they were pursued through fields and gardens. When he was first employed on the Windermere ferry, he was left alone on deck while the other men went to the Ferry Hotel.

Jack heard the thundering of hooves. Round the corner came a drove of horses belonging to the Logan family.

The young ferryman was supposed to fasten a chain across the lakeside end of the boat to contain any livestock. He paniced and darted through a door into the covered area. Then he watched, with lower jaw drooping, as the horses clattered across the deck—straight into the lake. 'Soon they were swimming in all directions.'

The ferry was always within hailing distance of the steamboats which maintained the Lakeside-Bowness-Waterhead service.

One morning, outward bound from Lakeside, a member of the crew noticed that a man was gazing sorrowfully over the side. He said that his wrist watch had fallen into the water when the strap broke. The watch was of sentimental value.

The crewman told him not to worry. 'Give me your name and address. When we clean t'lake out at t'back-end of t'year, I'll get it back for you.'

The passenger said: 'Don't be silly; nobody cleans out Windermere.' The sailor insisted he cleaned out the lake and, pointing to the flanking hills, he said: 'That's where we put all t'muck.'

Ower Kirkstone

Kirkstone is the Lake District at its greyest, sharpest, knobblest. It's a primeval scene of knolls and tumbling becks. Harriet Martineau, in her shilling guide for Victorian visitors, wrote; 'Near at hand, all is very wild. . . and the Kirkstone mountain has probably mists driving about its head.'

When I first knew the *Travellers' Rest,* a low white building on what appears to be a ledge cut out of the rock, it was the home of the Atkinsons, who had bought it in 1914. They lived between walls which are three feet thick and under a heavy slate roof.

The Atkinsons were proud to own the third highest licensed premises in England. (First and second places in the list are taken by *Tan Hill Inn,* on what used to be the Westmorland-Yorkshire border, and Derbyshire's *Cat and Fiddle*).

At Kirkstone, Pat Leighton the postman was blown over a wall, but was not unduly upset by the the experience. This Postman Pat was still delivering mail on his 81st birthday.

Kirkstone is in a world of mists. Snow covers the high slopes for over a month of the year. When slithering down Kirkstone one recent winter, I passed a car which had a young man in the driving seat and his friend sitting on the bonnet, bouncing to give the vehicle maximum grip. They deserved to get to the top, though I shuddered to think how many tenets of the Highway Code they had violated.

Professor John Wilson (better known as the writer Christopher North) crossed Kirkstone in January, 1816 when the body of a lad who had lost his way was being brought down. On that walk to Ambleside, the Professor walked OVER two gates.

Lord Lonsdale travelled by horse-drawn coach as he made for Grasmere Sports, and in August, 1895, he had the company of the German Emperor. Presumably they, unlike the common coach passengers of the time, were not asked to walk on the steepest gradients.

A visitor to the *Travellers' Rest* left the following verse:

He surely is an arrant ass,
Who pays to ride up Kirkstone Pass;
For he will find, in spite of talking,
He'll have to walk—and pay for walking!

The grey, dowly conditions of Kirkstone are endued by many sheep. The founder of a mini-bus service in Lakeland who wished to give it a memorable name recalled an adventurous crossing of Kirkstone and called his new transport service—Mountain Goat.

Bill Robson

I knew Bill Robson best a quarter of a century ago. It was a good time for bird-watching.

Ticking off species had not become a game. The countryside was not over-run with naturalists, nor had ornithology been commercialised to the extent of today, when birds are big business. A professional bird-watcher who blinks resembles a cash-register.

We watched birds in the old-fashioned way, entranced by their form, colour and movement. Birds were not so many items to be punched into a computer.

Bill Robson farmed near Appleby on six days each week. On the seventh day, he not so much rested from his labours as got dressed up for natural history. He was never casually dressed—or 'in his muck', as we say. His shirt had a tie attached to it. He wore a cap with the neb at the front, not at the side or back, as when tending cattle.

One of his old pals in natural history, who specialised in recording the sounds of birds, carried on the Victorian tradition of wearing a dark suit 'in the field'.

Bill and I once met him thus attired, and with a shirt that had an old-fashioned wing-collar, as we crossed some marshy ground in driving rain and mist. Bill recognised that naturalists were never slovenly in their dress but he suspected his friend was either over-doing things or trying to wear out his wedding suit.

I would call at Bill's farm in time for a cup of coffee provided by Ethel, his wife. Then off we'd go—on to the high Pennines for ravens, buzzards and peregrines, down the Eden Valley for oyster-catchers, grey geese or whooper swans [depending, of course, on the season] and into the Lake District for some deer-watching, a variation on the bird theme.

Bill had been doing this for so long I am sure he was on nodding terms with some of the birds he watched and ring ouzels reported to him when returning in March to their nesting places in the gills. Bill, given permission to enter the Warcop Army range, found that a wheatear pair were nesting down the barrel of an old tank which had been set up as a target.

In those days, before the bird protection laws were tightened, we would clamber to the rowan tree nest of a buzzard pair and see the chicks at the feathered stage, but with down still adhering to their heads, giving the impression they were wearing balaclava helmets.

We removed a hair from beside the eye of a nestling raven. That eye had become opaque. A one-eyed raven would not have lasted long in the grim setting of the High Pennines.

That day, Bill left his best setting-off crook propped against the cliff below the nest. When he returned for it, the crook had been taken. He saw it during the following week—being held by a farmer at the local auction mart. Bill, a somewhat shy man, could not bring himself to claim it from its new owner.

I associate Bill particularly with the ring ouzel, which he called 'mountain blackbird', the cock bird being just like a blackbird but with a white crescent on its chest.

Arriving in March from wintering grounds on the Atlas Mountains of North Africa, this species favours narrow rocky gills, also valleys with steep sides and tumbling becks.

As a bird-watcher, Bill 'had his eye in' for ouzels. Unerringly, he found the nesting areas. He knew potholes, shafts and levels where pairs nested in peace and security. The most unusual nesting area was on an aluminium ledge in the fuselage of a bomber aircraft which crashed during the war.

Back at home, Bill painstakingly wrote up his notes. He suffered from angina. On each excursion, he went through what he called 'my pain barrier'. He died, as he surely would have wished, while on a solo visit to the high fells, looking for a favourite alpine plant.

Bill had so many friends—in farming and natural history—that

Warcop's redstone church was packed for the funeral. His old bird-watching pal was still wearing the crow-black suit in which he bestrode the hills.

The Artful Dodger

It was a case of One Woman and her Dog. Katy Cropper, star of a local sheepdog trial, gave a series of cool, clear whistles—a sort of canine morse code. Her collie's response was crisp and immediate. Go left! Go right! Stop! Come on! The traditional commands were simple, unemotional.

A group of Swardles, straight off t'fell, was persuaded to take an unsheep-like course, between hurdles, round a post, into a pen. When the task was done, in a few minutes, the most spirited of the sheep leapt out of the pen and made off, as straight-necked as a fell fox.

The keenest spectators were other sheepdogs, one of which was being restrained by its master through the simple device of slipping the crook of his stick round its collar.

Lakeland farming as we know it today would be impossible without the collie, this Artful Dodger of the Fells. For the farmer needs a quick reliable way of rounding up sheep from hundreds of rocky acres.

Nowadays he has a motorised trike or one with four wheels, each model coming with 'balloon tyres', to give him quick access to the fellsides, but 'at the end of the day'—as nearly everybody says—the dog is needed to control the sheep. They are not likely to respect the authority of a clanking piece of machinery.

Years ago, the collie was almost as wild as a herdwick sheep. The dog was rarely patted and never allowed in the house. It was on the farm staff—there to work! When it was not working, it was chained up.

Some relaxation in the old attitudes has come with mechanisation. The modern collie responds to whistles from a farmer who is driving a Land Rover or van behind the flock.

The dog rides pillion on one of those noisy little trikes, successors of the Lakeland fell pony, which the modern shepherd finds indispensable (as well as fun) on the fells.

Man and dog are transported up a hitherto lonely fellside in a fug of exhaust fumes. Does the dog feel queezy after being driven at 50 miles an hour and more, then taken across a rough pasture, through a beck and up a slope covered with rush-bobs?

It's a dog's life from January to December but in late summer and early autumn—from what used to be haytime to the sheep sales—a dog that's 'worth owt' becomes a star at the sheepdog trials.

Up at Seathwaite, the wettest inhabited spot in England, the Edmondsons attend to their sheep while the dogs use up their surplus nervous energy running backwards and forwards on the walltops, their bright eyes missing nothing.

Faithful old dogs spend their years of redundancy sleeping on the flags in front of the farmhouses. Does a Cumbrian collie chase sheep in its dreams?

In autumn, the collies gather sheep for dipping, then for tupping. The terrain tests the stamina of the sheepdog. Some rough grund has rock which is hard enough to cut the pads. A too-eager collie might break a leg.

At the height of the growing season, bracken grows as tall as a man and a dog works blind in a mini-jungle of fronds which take on a bronze hue with the declining year.

A farmer I met in Girt Langdale was happy to chat about collies. He reckoned he knew a thing or two about them. We stood looking at the grandeur of a local hill, across which a patch of sunlight—a stray beam from the riven clouds—was travelling.

Said I: 'I suppose you've been up that fell scores of times.'

Said he: 'Nay—but dog hes!'

Mermaid at Cartmel

It was unmistakably Cartmel. A curious extension to the lantern tower of the old Priory shouted to be noticed. Here was an example of medieval economy, a chance to do something on the cheap at a time when the building fund was under strain.

On to the old lantern tower went a square belfry tower—set diagonally. It gives the Priory a jaunty appearance.

Some of the locals of the fifteenth century must have tut-tutted when the builder defied convention, but the tower endures. So does most of the original masonry of a Priory which, though suffering at the Dissolution of the Monasteries, was soon back in use, its roof restored, now serving as the parish church.

Entering the building on a stormy day, when its capacious roof was being used by day trippers as an umbrella, I made directly for the wooden shelf on which reposed two loaves of bread. This was not the modern, squared and sliced type of bread but a loaf that was rounded, baked locally with love.

Someone left £5 'to be laid out in bread and distributed to the most indigent housekeepers of this parish every Sunday for ever.' The number of loaves needed was incalculable. I made some inquiries. The bread—now symbolic—is replaced once a month and the old loaves are distributed in a way that would have appealed to St Francis of Assisi. They are fed to the ducks, which may arguably float lower in the water than the average mallard.

I was the 1,759th visitor that month, as recorded on a special calculator. The BBC had just been filming one of the tombstones which formed part of the floor. The stone that took the television producer's fancy commemorated a young man who was drowned on Lancaster Sands (Morecambe Bay).

Cartmel is almost surrounded by water. The 'land of Cartmel' juts out into the Bay and is flanked by two lively rivers, the Leven and Winster.

In addition, a curious little river known as the Eea, which is Old English for water, rises on Newton Fell and flows down a sweet and sour valley, with limestone to the east and slates to the west. The Eea eventually loops round Cartmel Priory. I asked the volunteer attendant here about the pronunciation of Eea. She said, flatly, 'ay'.

I was looking for a mermaid in Cartmel Priory. It had been shown to me by Canon Dickinson a dozen years ago. And there she was, carved on one of the misericords, those brackets on the choir stalls on which a monk might loll during the long services.

The mermaid has two tails and the obligatory comb and mirror. How was it that such a seductive creature appeared in a religious setting where the denizens were men?

She represents the lusts of the flesh which the monks should avoid at all costs, as indicated by the outline of a fish (symbol of Christianity) which is in the course of swimming away from her.

Disciples of John Peel

I've never been one for field sports. I did go fox-hunting, Lakeland-style, one January day—but I didn't see a fox. The Ullswater pack was meeting at Hartsop when the fells were bonneted with cloud. Hoping to write an article about fell foxes, I quizzed Joe Weir, the huntsman.

Joe's patience soon ran out. Turning to me, he snapped: 'Thee git into t'cigarette line.' I joined the few fag-smoking supporters.

Another time, attending the opening meet of the Blencathra in the days when the Master was Sir Percy Hope, I attended the local inn as someone announced he would sing *John Peel.*

The subject, Lakeland's most famous huntsman, was said to be 78 years old when he died in 1854. Hunting, usually on horseback, from his farm near Caldbeck, he directed his energies mainly against the straight-necked foxes of the Skiddaw range.

The song, inspired by a tune, which reverses the usual order of composition, was written by John Woodcock Graves, who greatly respected John Peel. It seemed appropriate to the occasion, for Peel's old Caldbeck pack was absorbed by the Blencathra.

I switched on a tape-recorder to capture the special quality of a local performance of the hunting ballad. The singer did well—for a couple of lines. Then his voice wavered and became silent. He'd forgotten the words!

Over 30 years ago, I researched the song about John Peel, trying to sort out fact from legend. At about that time, the magazine *Cumbria* organised a competition for a good Lakeland anthem. The judges were Sir Percy and Andrew Sievewright, organist at Carlisle Cathedral.

Eventually, we met round a piano in a local hotel to try out the short-list before an adjudication was made. It was a good time to get the impressions of the judges of the famous Cumberland ballad.

Sir Percy joyfully rendered a few lines of the song. Andrew commented: 'It has the strong simplicity of true folk music. . . It is a kind of chant whose intensity increases as the song proceeds, and it is memorable.'

John Peel's body may lie a-mouldering in the grave but, through the song, his soul—like that of the American, John Brown—goes marching on.

Grange and the Holy Well

A grange was a monastic farm. The Austin canons of Cartmel had one of their farms by Morecambe Bay. To reach it, they crossed a limestone hill and descended a rocky hillside, at the base of which was just a sliver of level ground against which the high tide smacked its lips.

So it was for centuries. The situation was transformed by piped water, which made residential life tolerable at this suntrap on the north Lancashire coast.

That and the Furness Railway which, coming in 1857, stabilised the coastline and restrained the Morecambe Bay tides. The railway company had tourism in mind when they built a somewhat fanciful station. The place became known as Grange-over-Sands. It sounded better than Grange-over-Mud, an allusion to the estuary of the Kent.

To the west of Grange stands Humphrey Head which, with St Bees, is the only high ground beside the sea from Wales to Scotland.

Visitors to the headland were not looking for sea views. They suffered from gout and other diseases of rich living. The springwater at the Holy Well, though 'bracky' [to quote a local man] was said to work wonders. The fact that it tasted foul was to its advantage. Medicine has to be nasty to do you good.

At Grange, the *Crown Hotel* catered for tourists. Then, in 1866, the *Grange Hotel* was built, with 70 rooms and a swimming bath filled with sea water. No one in his or her right mind swam in Morecambe Bay.

The Holy Well of Humphrey Head has become well-known again. Much of the headland has become the property of the Cumbria Wildlife Trust. Visitors are bound to taste the water, as a matter of interest. The well is less important now that medicine has provided many tasteless but powerful pills and potions...

Lots of Ravens

New-look, high-tech displays have transformed Tullie House at Carlisle. When I first ventured there, the place had a Victorian hangover, with innumerable glass-fronted cases and a conspicuous smell of furniture polish. I liked the place.

It was my pleasure to browse in the natural history section, under the beady eyes—literally the beady eyes—of typical Lakeland birds and beasts. I was especially fond of a raven. It had a solemn expression and plumage of undertaker black.

A 'stuffed' raven is a poor substitute for the real thing—a bird soaring on the updraught from a cliff edge, looking like a burnt fragment from a November bonfire. Young Wordsworth, living in the Hawkshead district, knew all about ravens and their proclivity for nesting in awkward places.

He wrote...

Oh! when I have hung
Above the raven's nest by knots of grass
And half-inch fissures in the slippery rock
But ill-sustained, and almost (so it seemed)
Suspended by the blast that blew amain,
Shouldering the naked crag.

It is not vital to dangle from cliff-edges when watching ravens. Happily, the bass-baritone croaking of the species is heard throughout the Lakeland fell country. An excited bird flings itself on its back and flies upside down for a spell, as though revelling in the sheer joy of life.

Fell-walkers see Old Croaky, which is distinguishable from the carrion crow by its large size and wedge-shaped tail. When deer-watching with Mike Hitchmough, of Kendal, in what a mutual friend calls 'Lakeland's Empty Quarter', I have found myself having to decide whether to keep my binoculars on a small party of hinds or watch a raven perched near its twiggy nest on the steepest part of the crag just behind the deer.

When visiting Tullie House, I would rap a knuckle on the door of the natural history curator's room and soon be in deep conversation with Ernest Bleazard, an avid raven-watcher. Ernest had counted sixty ravens at one winter roost.

He showed me pellets collected from near a nest. These 'castings' contained sheep wool and bones. The stomach of a Borrowdale raven found dead contained wool, grass, bone fragments and 16 rough pieces of quartz, comparable in its variety with the contents of a small boy's pockets.

Say it with Flowers

I've usually thought of the name Pendragon as a bit of medieval romance. And I've never wholly believed that wild boar were to be found on Wild Boar Fell. More likely they'd be snuffling in the oak and beech forest of Mallerstang. The tusk of one of them is kept under lock-and-key at Kirkby Stephen.

These thoughts jostled for attention as I drove into the Eden Valley on my way to Arthuret, in North Cumbria, where I had been invited to attend a flower festival.

Arthur Raistrick, North Country historian, used to laugh as he explained why some of the placenames were bound to be wrong. When the first Ordnance party arrived to make maps, they did not know the area well. West Country soldiers chatted to dialect-speaking Westmerians about placenames. Just imagine it!

Arthur—King Arthur, not Dr Raistrick—does bob up here and there in Cumbria. Near Penrith is Arthur's Round Table, a pretty name for something incomparably ancient. It lies close to but far away in spirit from the mighty M6.

Jonty Wilson, the blacksmith of Kirkby Lonsdale, theorised that you might trace the route taken by Arthur and his knights with reference to *Black Horse* pubs. The black horse, said Jonty, was sacred to the Celtic folk. Perhaps it is a distant folk memory that deters many of us from eating horse-flesh.

When I attended the flower festival at Arthuret, I found myself surrounded by displays dealing with aspects of the Arthurian legend. According to the latest of many theories about the Celtic King, he lived and died and his head was buried—Celtic style—at Arthuret.

No one was claiming anything definite about Arthur's local associations, of course, and—in any case—the anxious representative of West Country tourism had been quoted as saying that Arthur is of much greater value [in cash terms] as a legend than as historical fact.

I did hear frequent mention of Professor Norma Goodrich, from America. Her ideas about Arthur's association with the most northerly flourish of Cumbria had been supported by no less than *Burke's Peerage*.

Arthuret Church was thronged with folk. There was, overall, a friendliness—a geniality—with a mixed burring of Cumbrian and Scottish voices. The Rector's small son played some organ pieces, which provided a soothing background to much gossiping as old friendships were renewed.

I joined a party following the Rector, John Higgins, on a tour of the floral displays. He put across the 'balanced' view of Arthur. Definite proof is awaited.

I listened spellbound as he told the old, old story, plucked from the Dark Ages that followed the Roman occupation and somewhat romanticised as the centuries passed—a story about Arthur, his sword Excalibur, his knights and the round table, with feminine, and the hint of an adulterous relationship, provided by Guinevere.

It was a little tongue-in-cheek. A programme note by Pat Drysdale cheerfully acknowledged 'the very fact that there are few written records from the Dark Ages; this makes the Arthurian Legend fertile ground for creative expression.'

And create they did! The artefacts included a large piece of bog-oak, from the old forest smothered by peat: it was rightly said to be the oldest object on view in the Church.

The spirit of Arthur lives on in the county name—Cumbria, from the name of a Celtic tribe, whose tongue had the Welsh lilt about it. Consider, if you think of Arthur's day, two of our most noble fells—Helvellyn and Blencathra. Some major rivers, including Derwent, Eden and Esk, have kept their Celtic names.

Let me return to Arthuret, at flower festival time. As I sipped tea and demolished a sweet biscuit in a marquee pitched in the graveyard, a shiver passed down my spine.

Could Professor Goodrich be right? Was Arthur's head interred at Arthuret?

Might it be lying somewhere under this very tent wherein we were celebrating, with tea and biscuits, Arthur's return to Cumbria?

Dick's Wooden Leg

Fifty years ago, as the Allied armies swept through Italy, Dick Hilton—a soldier from northern England—was one of those unfortunate enough to tread on an anti-personnel mine. He was grievously wounded.

When, in due course, Dick set foot once again in his beloved Lake District, his sight and hearing were impaired and he moved about with the aid of—a wooden leg.

Dick was working as a youth hostel warden when I first knew

him. He settled eventually at the village of Newby, beside the road from the West Riding of Yorkshire to Kendal. Here his casual approach to housekeeping came close to wiping out the Clapham church choir during a break on their innocent errand of singing carols round the village.

How could this happen? Dick's main hobby was colour photography. He did all his own processing. Inviting the choir into his feebly-illuminated living room, he offered them wine. Some of the choristers complained that the 'wine' was bitter. Had it 'gone off?'

The visitors had actually been sipping photographic developer. Dick had re-cycled a wine bottle, filling it with a chemical from his dark-room. The choristers diluted the stuff by drinking copious quantities of tap water.

Despite a rigid leg, Dick continued to live the sporting life, including potholing. His boistrous activities were a challenge to the young and struggling National Health Service, who did manage to keep pace with his demands for new wooden legs.

If I decided on impulse to visit some remote spot in Lakeland, I'd sometimes call on Dick and invite him to join me. Dick immediately stopped whatever household task he was doing.

One Saturday morning, he'd been spring-cleaning the living room and most of the furniture was arrayed in the yard. It was returned in such a hurry as he prepared to join me on a visit to Lakeland that we left the house resembling a warehouse.

That day our destination was the summit plateau of High Street, with an easy approach from Haweswater. I have a clear mental picture of Dick negotiating the ridge. I fancy I can still hear the *thwack, plonk, thwack, plonk,* of booted foot and wooden leg.

Dick enjoyed visiting Walney Island, near Barrow-in-Furness, where he left some unusual footmarks in the sand. Wherever we went, he draw exclamations of admiration for his pluck. He got a loud 'by gad' from the ex-RAF officer through whose mini-estate we passed to reach Jim Ellwood's wild goose reserve by the Duddon Estuary.

In autumn, Bill Grant gave us overnight accommodation east of Coniston Water. At bedtime, I said: 'Goodnight, Dick.' He replied: 'Goodnight.' Dick's last job each day was to unstrap his wooden leg. Before I dozed off, I heard it clatter on to the floor.

Next morning, we were up and about in mist-shrouded Grizedale Forest, above Coniston Water, listening to the hoarse roaring of red stags.

Dick, an indomitable cyclist, died when he was involved in a road accident near Kirkby Lonsdale one Christmas. He had been up bright and early. There was no 'liggin' i' bed' for Dick.

His pleasure was to cycle through a splendid tract of Lakeland or the Yorkshire Dales. Bystanders saw a man, his bike—and a trusty wooden leg.

Slingsby's Chimney

When Cecil Slingsby was 77 years old, he startled some fellow walkers in the Lake District by springing on to a drystone wall. He balanced on a capstone with all the agility of an alpine goat.

This stocky and bearded Yorkshireman had kept himself subtle by testing himself on the Lakeland crags. In his prime, he led many a demanding climb. Slingsby's Chimney, a classic route on Scafell, was named after him.

Slingsby was born at Carleton-in-Craven, near Skipton, in 1849. He earned his daily bread in the family textile concern. It was from Carleton that he set off to climb—in the Lake District, the Alps and Norway. Slingsby is the 'father' of Norwegian climbing and, noticing that the peasants got about in winter on what were known as ski's, he took up ski-ing as a sport, and popularisted it in the Alps.

Slingsby sometimes went potholing, with a hempen ladder and a candle stuck on a bowler hat. But his real world was that of living rock and swirling mist. He and his friends, among them Haskett Smith, John Robinson, Charles and Laurence Pilkington, Solly and Norman Collie, formed a gloriously informal group who climbed for fun.

He opened up Norway to the climber through the appeal of his book *Norway: the Northern Playground*. He entertained Norwegians at his English home. One Christmas, when as usual he met climbing friends at Wasdale Head, Slingsby took along several Norwegians. He asserted: 'The best blood which we possess, we have derived from our 'fore-elders', the Vikings of Scandinavia.'

He was an exceptional climber, with the ability to 'read' the rock ahead. He was still climbing on Pillar Rock and Gimmer Crag when he was 'turned seventy'. Slingsby's daughter, Eleanor, with whom I corresponded for many years when editing *The Dalesman*, married the alpine climber Geoffrey Winthrop Young.

When I last chatted with Eleanor—then a very old but still charming lady—she told me some lovely stories from her childhood, including the time she accompanied her father to a local house.

An argument about religion was raging. The old grandfather who had been sitting silently turned in his chair, sighed and remarked: 'If t'Prayer Book's reight, it's reight. If not—clap it on t'fire back.'

I can imagine Cecil Slingsby chuckling at a story like that.

Sty Head

Seathwaite, at the head of Borrowdale, is reputed to be the wettest inhabited spot in the country.

You must have heard the story of the visitor who, impressed by a rainfall figure which is greatly in excess of a hundred inches a year, asked: 'Does it always rain here?'

The farmer replied: 'Nay—it sometimes snaws.'

The fells around Seathwaite were dusted with snow when I set out for Great End, via Sty Head. Under my boots were traces of an old causeway which led over to Wasdale—a route followed by the pack-horse trains. Wordsworth called Sty Head a 'horse-road'.

At the highest point of the ancient track, it was crossed by another, from Great Langdale to Ennerdale via Esk Hause and Windy Gap. This way was transported pieces of volcanic tuff excavated at the Pikes and being moved to the coastal settlements for final shaping and polishing as the famous Cumbrian Stone Axe—an export enterprise of four thousand years ago.

The highest point of the Sty Pass to Wasdale is marked by a mountain rescue post. Here stands a stretcher-box. A former Wasdale shepherd now living at Hesket Newmarket told me that once a man was crossing to Borrowdale when there was a 'thunder-plash'. He squeezed into the long wooden box for shelter from the storm. He was unable to get out unaided.

Hours went by. The desperate man wondered if there would be any other travellers that day. At about eleven o'clock, someone sat on the box. What should the prisoner do? If he spoke, he would surely frighten away the person who might save him?

He had to risk it. There was a gasp when his hollow voice sounded from the depths of the stretcher box. The new arrival released the trapped man who now set about saving the life of his rescuer, lost on unfamiliar ground. He was conducted down to Seathwaite.

Sty Head, with its excessive rainfall, its tarn, mountain cyclists and sandwich-eating gulls, was on the route I followed one Remembrance Day when I had given up my plan to reach the summit of Great Gable in time for the annual service. Early snow had blocked the Honister Pass.

So I took the Sty Head route from Seathwaite. Strains of Vaughan Williams's *Antarctica Symphony* went through my mind as I struggled to the summit, reaching it with just enough time to admire the panoramic view under a clear blue sky.

I spent the first two minutes recovering my breath. The second two minutes passed in silent meditation for victims of war. For the third two-minute period I was self-indulgent, rejoicing that I was standing fractionally higher than the ant-like figures clustering round the war memorial on Gable.

Grey Geese

At Derwentwater, the mist was so thick I could taste it. A water-colour artist would have needed no more than washes of various shades of grey to capture sky, water, promontories and islets.

The lake was gunmetal grey. The back of a female merganser was grey; she tried to beat some life into the lake as she took flight. The farmyardy calls came from a flotilla of greylags, lying just off St Herbert's Island.

The last time I saw greylags on Derwentwater, both the adults and goslings were unable to fly. The seniors had moulted their flight feathers and the young were not yet at the stage of flight.

As Friars Crag was vacated by tourists, in the evening, the geese drifted warily to the shore, intent on grazing a local field. It was a strange sight—this procession of wary geese, leaving water to waddle like sailors across a popular footpath, thence up a steep bank to the chosen field.

The Lake Poets used the grey goose quill when they wrote. From the greylag, ancestor of our domestic geese, came feathers used on arrows shot from longbows in ancient battles.

The greylag died out as an English nesting species, only to be reintroduced by Jim Ellwood, of Millom, who got some Scottish eggs and, at his little reserve by the Duddon estuary, hatched them out under jungle fowl. I spent many an hour watching them. In winter, the geese were able to commute to the wild and, conversely, wild greylags began to use the reserve as a sanctuary.

I became familiar with his little wooden hut, and especially with the tea-making facilities. Jim could not understand why the breed took so long to become established in the wild until a freckle-faced farm lad remarked that nearly all his pals now had wild goose eggs in their collection.

Jim worked with WAGBI, the wildfowlers' organisation. He supported a scheme for introducing greylags to the tarns of Grizedale Forest.

'Good old Jim,' said the conservationists.

The farmers, who saw greylags in increasing numbers on their best grass, were not so enthusiastic.

Nobbut Sheep

We should be grateful to sheep for keeping the views open on the Lakeland fells. If they did not vary their diet of grasses and herbs by nibbling saplings, there'd be trees all over the place and fell-walkers who could not read maps properly would get lost.

In Lakeland, sheep come in three types—Swardles (or Swaledales, if you want the Sunday name), 'Erdwicks (or Herdwicks) and 'hawf bred 'uns', which is a genetic blend, a consequence of skilful management by the farmer or, alternatively, a liaison between an over-amorous male sheep that escaped from captivity and 'had its way' with some females.

Male sheep are known as tups (or tips, if you live in western Lakeland) and teearps (in the east). If a farmer says teeeaaarps, he's had too much to drink. Females are ewes or 'yows'.

Some people keep 'fancy sheep' like Jacobs, which are mottled, so that the wool needn't be dyed if the owner decides to make some warm but itchy clothes from his/her stock.

The Rare Breeds which are now very common include the Skiddaw Square Sheep (which used to be over-wintered in outside privies at the fellside farms) and the Borrowdale Lopsided Sheep (awkward-looking on level ground but comfortable when grazing on the steep slopes beside that famous valley).

Lakeland fell sheep were once flighty. As soon as your head appeared above the horizon, a couple of miles away, they were off like a straight-necked fox. In the popular areas, some sheep trail walkers, rather like gulls following ships at sea, waiting for the human visitor to toss away a piece of bread. Happily, most sheep stick to their own ground.

'They' do say the herdwick is descended from sheep from a galleon of the Spanish Armada wrecked off St Bees, but 'they' will say owt. Some people claim it was brought here by the Vikings. 'Appen. I think it's just a native crag sheep which has been improved, and titivated (using red rudd) to give it the appearance of a guardsman's jacket. A terrible lot of improvement took place last century.

The herdwick, which drinks in a love of its native fell with its mother's milk, and sneezes with annoyance if you picnic on its favourite patch of ground, would be a rare breed now if Beatrix Potter had not handed over some of the best fell farms in the Lake District to the National Trust and stipulated that the old herdwick stocks should be maintained.

I'm surprised she never wrote one of her books about a herd-wick. Perhaps she couldn't get a good name to go with it. Harry Herdwick or Horace Herdwick would sound daft.

A herdwick is a dark lile think when it's born and grows up into a sheep which has a face covered with white hair, resembling hoar frost. The wool may not be worth much to farmers but is first-rate insulation for the sheep and it turns over a hundred inches of rain a year. Herdwick legs are thick and well placed, like table legs, well suited to the gale-ridden heights. T'auld farmer said that herdwick mutton was Royal mutton, sweet and toothsome.

The Swaledale is popular because it's worth more that a herd-wick, though it's not as tough. Now and again, it needs a bit of herdwick blood to fit it for life in the rocky heart of Lakeland.

Some say it's a Yorkshire sheep, and some regard it as a Westmorland type. There are even people who claim it to be a type fixed in county Durham. They're all correct, in a way, for the Swaledale evolved on and around *Tan Hill Inn,* where three counties meet.

So there we are—over-run with sheep. If it wasn't for them keeping everything neat and tidy by champing at every living plant they find, our Lake District would be in a right draggly mess by now. And who wants to travel all the way from Cornwall to Cumbria, from Bedford to Blencathra or from Guildford to Gable if all that can be seen is a lot of trees and sky?

Quietest Ambleside

Charlotte Bronte's first visit to Ambleside, in 1850, was a tonic to her jaded spirits. This being Charlotte, a woman with restless fingers, she was soon scribbling down her thoughts in letter form, stating: 'My visit to Westmorland has certainly done me good.'

My latest visit to Ambleside, just before Christmas, had the same effect. People were thin on the ground. I seemed to have the streets to myself and, in St Mary's Church I was solitary but not lonely. Then the primary school choir arrived to rehearse a carol—to an audience of one.

St Mary's, its spire attaining a height of 180 ft., rises in Victorian splendour from a knoll which was an islet in the days when Windermere lapped and fretted much further up the valley than it does today. The church appeared in a time of religious certainty, when issues were either white or black, with no shades of grey.

The church was unheated on the day of my visit. Soon I had the heart-warming experience of listening to the young choristers. One or two children arrived. I was about to say that they 'drifted in', but that is not the way of children. It was more of a cheerful saunter.

I heard two dozen pairs of shoes and a hub-bub of conversation; they brought life back to George Gilbert Scott's grand design of 1854. The children then sang joyfully and confidently, without a trace of 'nerves', which in my young days were a potentially embarrasing affliction and led to forgotten lines and much sobbing.

Down by the Brathay, I listened to the river's song and thought of char—not a cup of tea, I hasten to add, but a fish which normally lives in the depths of Windermere but, in late November, runs up into the river to spawn. The eggs are deposited in the gravel beds. Some eggs will be swept away by the scouring water and others regarded as food by creatures of the river, not forgetting ducks.

Camden, one of the first visitors to Lakeland to set down his thoughts and discoveries, called the char 'a sort of golden alpine trout'. The fish are descended from a stock which once migrated but became land-locked during the Ice Age. A cock fish in its breeding condition has a bright red belly.

100

The Fleming family sent 'potted char' from Lakeland to a relative in London. In the good old days at Brockhole, the National Park centre near Windermere, I was once offered a sliver of char, with such a delicate taste it was difficult to isolate it from the rest of an excellent buffet meal.

The Bridge House, in which the womenfolk from Ambleside Hall are thought to have sat on hot summer days, protecting their delicate skin from direct sunlight, now had frost in its joints. The last folk to live here, in 1901, were Chairy Rigg and his wife. He repaired chairs and sold ferns. Victorian coach drivers were fond of telling their passengers that the house on the bridge was built by a Scotsman who was trying to avoid paying ground rent!

The nearby road bridge was being renovated. A web of scaffolding and wooden planks allowed men to work dryshod. With an arch of masonry above their heads they would at least keep dry if it rained.

The spirit of winter was evident in the absence of a queue of people at Dove Cottage, Grasmere. I stood in the dark, fire-warmed parlour of the Cottage and referred to Dorothy's *Journal* entries for Christmastide, 1801. On December 24: 'Still a thaw. William, Mary and I sat comfortably round the fire in the evening and read Chaucer. Thoughts of last year. I took out my old journal.'

Christmas Day was nothing special. 'We received a letter from Coleridge,' wrote Dorothy.

Butty Stops

A butty stop, as devised by Bob Swallow, is just what you'd imagine it to be—a pause during an outdoor excursion for food and drink. The butty, a glorified sandwich, represents the main course of a standard meal. The 'extras' range from a slab of chocolate to a bunch of grapes.

These teeth of mine have champed their way through hundreds of ham sandwiches. Once, memorably, I dined on Walney Island, off Barrow-in-Furness, a yard or two above sea level. I had taken some Bowland friends to Walney, anxious to introduce them to my old friend Walter, the warden, and his myriad gulls, eiders and terns.

You could always tell when the eggs were hatching because then the birds showed the greatest stress, diving on anyone who ventured near the nests. Walter's battered trilby hat was soon plastered with white from well-directed bird excrement.

When butty time arrived, I opened my small haversack and brought forth some sandwiches, with the customary ham filling, I settled down to eat. We were near the car, from which my guests brought forth half a hundredweight of equipment, furniture and tins containing food. They had a three-course meal on the sand dunes.

Another time, at low level, I was savaged by a pheasant. The chosen spot during a long walk was a grassy bank near a waterfall in a woodland situation. I had just lifted a Scotch egg from my butty-box when a pheasant flew in, determined to have the egg. I had literally to push it away with the box and during the tussle the egg rolled into the beck.

In Lakeland proper (the high fells) I have eaten tomato sandwiches in the rain on High Street, cheese sandwiches in the snow on Harter Fell, ham-and-cheese sandwiches on Gable, and plain ham sandwiches almost everywhere else. When Colin completed his Wainwrights, I (born and bred a Methodist) moistened my lips with whisky on Fleetwith Pike (the others had generous drams).

What began as a plain butty-stop has been ritualised by Bob. He distinguishes between major and minor butty-stops, two of each per expedition, to the amazement of some friends who 'eat nowt' during their Lakeland outings. Having spent a long summer's day on Glaramara and adjacent fells, we tottered (almost dehydrated) into Seathwaite for supplementary refreshment in the form of ice cream.

At the start of one new year, during a mopping-up excursion for Wainwrights, we called at Ike's farm in Newlands Valley and had Christmas cake with a lile drink o' summat a bit stronger than tea.

Dining conditions may leave a lot to be desired. On Helvellyn, the wind was chilly enough to put ice crystals in the blood. Back o' Skiddaw, as I champed the regulation-size ham sandwiches, I watched lumps of peat drying and cracking on my boots. Bob awards marks—one to five—for the view when 'buttying'. Only once has the highest number of points been awarded—and that was in Stan's front room on the outskirts of Cockermouth. Outside, a fierce battle was taking place between the elements. We were refugees from the storm.

In the afternoon, during a 'window' in the weather pattern, we light-heartedly took in a fell near Buttermere. We were light-hearted partly because we had little to carry, having left our rucksacks, butty boxes and thermos flasks in the car, which we parked near the lake.

It's only Catbells

Bob proposed a light-hearted saunter. We inquired which peak he had in mind. 'It's only Catbells,' was his reply. When we parked the car near Hawes End, it crossed my mind that we might even leave the engine running. We would not be away for long.

The wind, fresh from sweeping the snowfields of the high ground, gave buoyancy to the ravens which for a time seemed to enjoy our company. They put on an air display which included flipping on their backs, then back again. Their bass-baritone voices drifted through the thin air.

The well-defined path led us up the spine of Catbells, offering a view of Derwentwater, grey as gunmetal under leaden clouds. Southwards, around Seatoller, the riven clouds allowed shafts of light to appear, like spotlights at a theatre, coaxing colour from a winter-weary landscape.

Our feet crunched on ice. But 'it's nobbut Catbells.' We would soon be returning to car-comforts.

Bob surveyed Lakeland from a summit crusty with ice and thought Castle Crag looked tempting—and so near! 'It's only Castle Crag. . .' We descended to Grange-in-Borrowdale. I had a glimpse, among trees of Brackenburn, once the Lakeland home of the novelist Hugh Walpole, and thought pleasurably of my latest visit to Brackenburn, when I sampled water—the clearest, coldest water in Lakeland—which had been drawn from the heart of Catbells.

Soon we were queuing to climb the zig-zag scree slope to the summit of Castle Crag (a butty-stop graded 'four' on our special scale relating to the view). Up there, with a lazy wind trying to force its way through us, we beheld the great oak forest of Borrowdale and the lake.

Bob fancied doing the odd peak on the other side of Borrowdale. What had he got in mind? 'It's only Grange Fell. . .'

Then Bob decided we would make a bee-line for the car. Apart from the fact that all self-respecting bees were tucked up in their hives, waiting for spring, there was the small matter of Derwentwater. Was Bob suggesting that we use up the rest of our energy while swimming across with rucksacks clasped in our teeth?

'It's only Derwentwater. . .' The path led us slithering downwards, among the trees, to the Borrowdale road. Bob had a boat crossing in mind, a romantic idea, though romance was shredded when we discovered the penultimate boat, in the direction we desired, had just left the jetty.

'It's only an hour before the last boat comes...' said Bob. 'It's only blooming cold,' said his semi-mutinous friends. Apart from having to wait in a refrigerated airstream, that evening was magical. We watched the dying sun give Skiddaw's snow fields a pinkish hue. We were entertained by ducks and watched a flypast of greylags.

On the other shore of Derwentwater, we walked stiff-legged from the boat, and blundered along a path at the 'edge o' dark.' Bob said: 'It's only half a mile...' No one replied. Climbing little Catbells had been quite an effort.

In a Few Words

Of a rather posh man who walked by without speaking: 'Some folks is eddicated till they're ignorant.'

A wayside pulpit notice had one word: 'Think'. Someone wrote underneath: 'Or Thwim.'

After a difficult customer had left the small shop, the owner said to his assistant: 'They're all queer 'cept thee and me. And thou's queer sometimes.'

Motorist driving into the forecourt of a garage: 'Thursa laal naffle a yarside' (His car had a rattle at one side).

Sayings of the Dalesfolk

Heard in Wasdale: 'Ivvery parish had a different way of its own. Now it's all of a splutter.'

Farmer in Borrowdale (to his farm man, who has asked for a day off): 'Aye—but be back for milkin' toneet.'

Upper Lunesdale: 'Well, your family wean'd need mich help, wi' three gurt lads, big as house-ends and strong as waggin-hosses.'

Near Coniston: 'When we came here, ivverybody had a bit o' corn and a bit o' grass. Now nobody has nowt.'

Former Shepherd: 'I don't like mutton. I'se seen too many wicks in it.'

About the Ulverston Hiring Fair: 'If a farmer thowt somebody leuked like a big lump o' labour, he'd go and see if he could hire him—for as little as he could.'

Borrowdale Farmer (to his servant lass who is fastening up her apron at the start of another day's work): 'Nay—fasten it when thou's coming downstairs—and lowse it again when thoo's going to bed.'

In Little Langdale: 'My fadder telled me folk die in bed so I should not spend much time there. T'bed didn't encourage you to dawdle; it had a straw mattress wi' a feather mattress on top.'

At Skelwith Bridge: 'Coffee pot was emptied yance a week. And we popped egg shells in to clean it.'

Near Glenridding: 'You can keep your farmhouse cookery. It was not as good as they mak oot. Farmers' wives'd git a great lump o' meat, boil it for Sunday, and we'd hev it cowd for t'rest o' t'week.'

JOHN PEEL AND SKIDDAW.

Little Langdale: 'We'd kill a sheep and eat t'best part on it, though if t'head were on t'small side we whanged it into t'dog hut... It were said of a good lamb that it should be cooked twice—yance on t'hill and yance in t'oven.'

Ned Tyson (to a doctor who met him in the street and asked him how he was): 'I'se nut telling thee. Last time thoo axed me I got a bill for seven and a tanner.'

Quarryman at Elterwater (who walked home on a dark night and, putting his hand out to detect a five-barred gate, was unlucky when it passed between two bars): 'It's fust time I knew mi nose was longer than mi arm.'

Lakeland Sights and Sensations

A is for ANIMALS. Especially sheep. The tips [males] have curving horns, like handlebars, which gives the farmer something to get hold of when he's attending to them.

B is for BROCHURES. They are shiny, colourful and packed with pictures of smiling people. The photographs, taken in full sunlight and with everlasting blue skies, cheer you up when it's raining.

C is for CLIMBERS. Identifiable by an absence of finger nails (which bestrew the rock ledges). Normally, climbers progress, an inch an hour, with a series of grunts. Don't feed the brutes while they're dangling from crags.

D is for DROPPINGS. Trillions of sheep droppings. In moorland situation, it is important (as Wainwright pointed out) not to confuse fresh droppings with ripe bilberries.

E is for EAGLE. That's the black spot against the cloud. If you're in doubt as to whether or not a large bird is an eagle, then it's a buzzard.

F is for FARMERS. For centuries, they've kept the National Park neat and tidy, with little thanks. A farmer never has a good or a bad year—it's always 'just middlin'.'

G is for GATEWAY. Farmers always manage to put it in the muddiest part of the field.

H is for HERDWICK. Lakeland's lile sheep. Frosty face and coarse woolly jacket. Unlike walkers, it never seems to get out of breath on the hills. It has a boring life—eight hours sleep, eight hours grazing, eight hours chewing the cud.

I is for INFORMATION. Tons of free or cheap info are available at Information Centres, which are periodically raided by school parties.

J is for JEMIMA PUDDLE-DUCK and the vast and lucrative Beatrix Potter business. You'll find real-life Jemimas and Peter Rabbits in every part of the district. On Windermere, Jemima has cross-bred with Aylesburys and there's a few hundred of Peter's descendants in every parish.

K is for KIRKSTONE and all the other high passes of Lakeland, where a visitor can go mountaineering without leaving the car. Wrynose and Hardknott Passes are not, as one bemused visitor thought, a short cut from Ambleside to Blackpool.

L is for LAKE. There's only one—Bassenthwaite Lake. You'll not find 'lake' mentioned in any other name.

M is for MOTOR VEHICLE. A tin box on wheels. Note the packet of paper handkerchiefs on the ledge near the back window. Motor vehicles by the thousand arrive and depart at high speed via the Kendal by-pass, near which each bird and beast has developed a nervous twitch.

N is for NAPES NEEDLE. Like a large stone thorn in the side of Great Gable. Or a Stone Age space vehicle about to be shot into orbit. Napes Needle is often festooned with climbers. Graham Sutton wrote a short story called 'The Man Who Broke the Needle', about a climber who. . . But no, read it for yourself. . .

O is for OTLEY, JONATHAN, the 'father' of Lakeland guide book writers. Six million guides later, people are still finding things (the same things) to write about. Yawn, yawn.

P is for POSTMAN PAT, a lovable little character of television and children's books inspired by rural life in Old Westmorland. Pat's so busy he hasn't time to read all the postcards.

Q is for QUEUES. Mainly at toilets (hence the old saying: 'Mind your Ps and Qs') and the pay-desks of supermarkets.

R is for RAIN. Or 'liquid sunshine'. In the wettest season, people with brown tans are suffering from a bad attack of rust.

S is for SHEEP. Ubiquitous. Sheep invade gardens, where they have a partiality for rose bushes. They accept sandwiches and liquorice allsorts from visitors. At Rydal, given half a chance, they dine on the sacred Wordsworthian daffodils.

T is for THREE (SHIRES STONE), beside the Wrynose Pass. The stone is nowt o' t'sooart. Only 'Lancashire' is inscribed upon it. The Stone does stand (approximately) where Lancashire was on nodding terms with Cumberland and Westmorland.

U is for UNDERWATER EXPLORATION. Some people do it accidentally. The experts, with sophisticated breathing apparatus, try not to put their foot on the bottom and stir up the mud. In Windermere, rows of eels, at the entrances of their hidey-holes, look like soldiers on parade.

V is for VISITORS. Their presence has turned Heritage into Big Business—a business which stretches a point here and there for maximum commercial effect. Did Wordsworth really use after-shave lotion?

W is for WAINWRIGHT. Of Course. The Patron Saint of Fellwalkers is reviled by some but his books are an inspiration to many. Wainwright's work will live if only because he made us laugh.

X is for Xmas, a season which begins in Lakeland during the tourist season, with the sale of cards and calendars. Snow scenes are purchased in August sunshine/rain (cross out that which is not applicable).

Y is for YANWATH. And all the other curious, hard-sounding names attributed to the Norsefolk.

Z is for Zzzzzzzz. You must be worn out by now. It's time for a doze.

'Golf's a funny game, caddie.'
'Aye—but it isn't meant to be.'

Basic Cumbrian

HERE are three examples of broad Cumbrian in action:

A fiddler to some dancers: Noo me canny lads an' lasses, tak yer spots for a square eight reel. Than Ah'll strike up t'teun.

Invitation in a public house: Good mwornin! What ur ye gaen ta hev ta sup?

A prayer at Cockermouth Fair: Lword, when Thoo sees a publican watterin' his whiskey an' rum tull its varra wake, or sellin' slop-yeal ower agean, a durty trick, mak his reet arm drop doon streight be his-side an' div n't alloo 'im pooer ta lift it agean tull t'Fair's ower.'

Hardly anyone talks like this any more—if they ever did, for the quotations are from a written work, *Idylls of a North Country Fair* [Cockermouth], containing Cumberland prose and verse.

Here's a collection of Cumbrian words which, used sparingly, could give character to your speech:

Addle. If you are a wage-earner, then you addle brass [money].

Agist. A farmer addles a bit of extra brass by letting out some pastureland to his neighbour so he can graze his young cattle during the summer.

Amackily. It means 'fashionable', which is more than can be said for this strange word today.

Amaist. Slot this into a conversation now and again, in place of 'almost', and you'll be takken for a Cumbrian—for five seconds.

Ax. Not an implement but the process of inquiring—you might ax somebody the way to the bus station. (On Sunday, the parson might read a piece from the Ax of the Apostles).

Beck. Our word for what folk in t'softer South Country call a brook.

Birk. We share this word with Scotland; it means a birch tree.

Blebb'd. Or drank, as when you've downed a pint of yal [ale].

Boke. To be avoided in polite company. It's a belch.

Boutry. The Lakeland name for an elder tree. It's just as easy to say 'elder'.

Braffin. A horse-collar, still used annually at Egremont where they have a competition for gurnin [grinning] through a braffin.

Brant. It means steep. Relates to hillsides rather than yesterday's restaurant bill.

Brattl't. This signifies noise, which is a better word.

Brosson. If you're 'fair brosson', you've had too much to eat, though the word really means 'to burst'.

Bumblekite. The old name for a blackberry. My favourite 'blegging' country is near Wigton, where t'bumblekites seem twice as big as anywhere else.

Bummelt. You've bungled something!

Bump. Nothing to do with falling down steps. It's a coarse type of woollen yarn, the type of stuff produced in Kendal and distributed to the hand-knitters of the Dales.

Bus. Long before the infernal-combustion engine was invented and Mrs Diesel's favourite son was born, this word was used in Cumbria for—a kiss.

Cap. Lakeland farmers like caps wi' nebs on 'em. The word cap also means 'to surpass' such as when a boastful person says: 'I'll cap 'em aw [all].'

Cawkers. A set of 'irons' fitted to clogs, which were ideal weapons in a school playground. An adroit lad could raise some sparks by dashing his cawkered clogs against a flagstone.

Chow. A slang word for chew but in the Cumbrian context it means 'to grumble'.

Chimlay. The local way of saying 'chimney'. In Lakeland, round chimneys are common. They were the best way to use up assorted stones. Wordsworth is said to have liked them, so they must be aw reight.

Clag. This means 'to stick'. If you become clagged you've pushed too much dry food into your mouth. If the lane outside your house is claggy, its dirty and sticky after rain.

Clart. A close relative of 'clag', used for something which is dirty. Sometimes used for the amorphous mass periodically deposited by a cow.

Clash-ma-saunter. An endless telling of tales. Displaced by televised drivel.

Cleg. A horse fly, which has its own blood transfusion service. The first you know about it is when you feel a prick like a red-hot needle. And there's no cup of tea and biscuit to follow.

Crack. An easy-going, gossipy conversation. 'I'se just popped in for a crack'. Might last aw neet.

Cuddy. The Cumbrian name for a donkey.

Cwoartin'. The pre-marital stage, which used to last about two years. Modern youngsters cannot wait that long!

Cwoat. The Cumbrian word for a coat. That which belonged to the famous huntsman, John Peel, was of hodden grey (undyed wool).

Dezd. It means 'cold and stiff'.

Dobbie. A ghost, in the presence of which people feel dezd.

Dollop. A lump of food, such as poddish dumped on your breakfast plate.

Drokk'n hizzy. A drunken woman.

Eea. Means water and is used in the names of two rivers—the Ea (near Cartmel) and Eamont (the outflow of Ullswater).

Ehint. Anything that's behind you.

Fain. To be glad.

Farrow. When a pig delivers its young. If you want to sound well-read, you can talk about the 'parturient effort of the sow'.

Fash. Another word we share with our northern neighbours, the Scots, as with 'dinna fash yerself', or—stop worrying!

Fettle. The act of restoring something to its proper condition. A farmer 'fettles' a broken yat [gate].

Flammergasted. Taken aback or, as was written in the Bible, 'sore amazed'. A Mallerstang farmer says 'fair capped'.

Flait. Afraid. It's more than likely you'll be flait of ghosts, angry bulls and tax inspectors.

Gait. Not the sort to be fettled. This kind of gait [also known as a stint] is a unit of pasturage on a common pasture.

Gammerstang. It's just what it sounds like—a clumsy sort of person. [see the next entry].

Garrock. The local word for awkward.

Geuss. A goose, as in 'thoo's an oald geuss.' A gosling's known as a gezzlin.

Girt. Much more expressive than the standard English 'great'.

Gully. In Cumberland, it was a small round grating. Others used it for a kitchen bread knife.

Guff. A fool.

Gurn. See 'Braffin'. Gurn is what you do through it!

Helter. From halter—a horse collar. [Hev anudder leuk at 'Braffin'].

Hog. Not a pig but a weaned lamb. A Langdale farmer with a score of hogs is driving a small flock of sheep. He'd hev a divvel of a job to drive a small herd of pigs.

Ken. To know, as in 'D'ye ken John Peel?'

Keslop. A calf's stomach. When the calf had finished with it, the stomach was used in the cheese-making process.

Kezzlup-skin. A substance used in curdling milk when cheese-making [see Keslop].

Kirk, sometimes Kurk. It's the Cumbrian word for Church. Those who attend, the Kurk-fwoke, finish up in t'Kurk-garth [churchyard].

Kysty. A kysty person is one who is fastidious about food. Most kids are kysty if you let 'em git awa' wi' it.

Ley. The Cumbrian term for a scythe.

Lig. To lie down.

Lish. To get up and rush about.

Loup or Lowp. If you have enough energy left, you might loup [leap].

Lwonnin. Courting couples used to go down t'lwonnin [lane]. Now they have a week in Tenerife.

Lug. The old law mark of the Norse folk, involving the clipping of a sheep's ear, which led to the ear becoming known as lug. The lugs of naughty lads were once clattered [smacked]. Most lads, left alone, would nivver wesh ehint their lugs.

Maffly. Means 'childish'. Also applied to an an adult who has become mentally confused.

Midden. Where t'muck goes. At a house, it's mainly ash from the fire. On the farm, the midden is adjacent to the byre. Good muck from the wintering cows is spread across the land in spring as a fertiliser—and also to get rid of the stuff!

Miff-maff. Thoo's talking a lot o' nonsense.

Nobbit. Only.

Oald. Old. 'Theer ne feul [fool] like an oald feul.'

Onny. Any.

Poddish. Porridge, once a staple food at the majority of Cumbrian homes. In Kentmere, they liked it so thick a mouse might walk dry-shod across it.

Ranty. The name for someone who is thought to be mad.

Reedent. (Sometimes pronounced r'eedu'nt). The reedent person has become red-faced with temper.

Reedin. Scraping and cleaning intestines, such as those of a pig prior to making black puddings or sausages.

Reet. Right.

Rivin'. Usually relates to tearing, as with old clothes being torn up to be used as dusters. In Lakeland, rivin' is what they do with large pieces of slate, splitting them into narrow pieces for trimming and use as roofing material.

Scowp. A metal scoop, with a wooden handle at one side, used for many a job in a farmhouse, including emptying a set-pot. Put a long handle on a scowp, and you have just the thing for lifting silt from gutters or liquid manure from a 'middin'-pan'.

Skemmel. A long wooden form for a farmhouse kitchen. At mealtime, if you delayed reaching t'skemmel by a minute, the meal would be half over.

Slatter. Wet and dirty.

Slokk'n. Quenching the thirst.

Steg. The term for a gander, as in 'sturdit (stupid) ess a steg.'

Ta-gidder. Together. 'Ye go gay weel ta-gidder.'

Thibel or thrivel. A wooden stick used for stirring porridge (and whacking the mouse if it tries to walk dry-shod across it. See 'Poddish'). A similar sort of object was used for lifting clothes out of the set-pot on wash day.

Thrang. You're thrang when you have too many jobs for the available time.

Thrattles. Sheep droppings.

Tick. A parasite on a mammal. Sheep are dipped against ticks.

Tip. From the word 'tup', meaning a male sheep. Tip is the term generally used in western Lakeland. Posh farmers refer to a ram.

Twang. The native speech, 't'good oald Cummerlan twang.'

Wick. A person is wick if he/she is alive. It was said of a man aged 96: 'I reckon t'Almighty must hev forgitten 'im.'

Wrawlin'. Grumbling.
Wuslan'. Wrestling.
Yak. An oak tree.
Yat. A gate.
Yal. Served a pint at a time, the name meaning ale.
Yan. One. 'Tyson's yan o' t'best.'
Yance. Once. 'I yance axed tha.'
Yubben. The Cumbrian word for oven.

It's good to end this book on a homely note. Draw a chair up
to the fire—

> But here's ta iverybody's health
> Ne matter what their gender!
> An' may we offen meet agean
> Be this oald kitchen fender;
> In t'past we've hed a jolly life
> An' niver wisht ta mend it;
> Hooray! a rag-tag bob-tail lot
> We'll be tull we ur endit.

'My husband had
it made when
he finished
his Wainwrights.'

Castleberg Books by W R Mitchell

After You, Mr. Wainwright

An affectionate and amusing tribute to the master fell-walker. It also relates how several sufferers from Wainwrightosis climbed some of his favourite peaks. The book is dedicated to Betty, the widow of AW.

The sense of infectious fun is accompanied by Mitchell's observations on natural history, snippets of Lakeland lore, excerpts from Victorian guide books and wisdom gleaned from chats with farmers and shepherds.
—"Yorkshire Evening Post"

ISBN: 871064 65 1
£4.99

The Lost Village of Stocks-in-Bowland

Life in the upper Hodder valley of Bowland before a reservoir was built to supply the Fylde coast of Lancashire, including Blackpool and Fleetwood, with drinking water. Based on taped interviews with former residents. Illus. photographs and line drawings.

. . . very readable and interesting—"Nelson Leader"

ISBN: 1 871064 90 2
£5.60

Drystone Walls of the Yorkshire Dales

Taped interviews with drystone wallers in various parts of the Dales have provided much hitherto unpublished material. Also notes on folklore and natural history. Foreword by Richard Muir.

This is a splendid account of how walls are constructed without mortar and of the men who built them—"Lancashire Magazine"

ISBN: 1 871064 80 5
£5.20

Mr. Elgar and Dr. Buck

A 50 year long friendship between Edward Elgar and Charles William Buck of Giggleswick, in Yorkshire, was important in Elgar's transition from musician to composer. Foreword by Lady Barbirolli.

. . . the fact that this book is an indulgence is a point totally in its favour for the fun and detective work involved in the research and writing shines through every sentence. —"Westmorland Gazette"

ISBN: 1 871064 05 8 £5.60

Ribblehead Re-born

Ribblehead viaduct, with its 24 high arches, epitomises the spirit of the railway that crosses the High Pennines on its way from Settle to Carlisle. After a restoration costing £3 million, the viaduct now looks as smart as it did when the line was opened to regular passenger traffic in 1876.

ISBN: 1 871064 70 8 £4.99

Hotfoot to Haworth

Sub-titled "Pilgrims at the Bronte Shrine", this book deals with the astonishing growth of a literary cult surrounding the three talented Bronte sisters. The book is published as Haworth prepares to celebrate the centenary of the Bronte Society in 1993.

ISBN: 1 871064 75 9 £4.99

Yorkshire Laughter

Dozens of the best examples of the native wit and humour. Illustrations in line by IONICUS. Foreword by Freddie Truman, OBE.

ISBN: 1 871064 85 6 £4.99

A Popular History of Settle and Giggleswick

Fragments of history from a variety of sources presented in chronological order. From the Norman Conquest to the present day.

ISBN: 1 871064 95 3 £5.40

'Castleberg Publications', 18 Yealand Avenue, Giggleswick, Settle, North Yorkshire, BD24 0AY.